UNFULFILLED PROMISE

UNFULFILLED PROMISE

MEMORIES OF DONOGH O'MALLEY

PJ BROWNE

CURRACH
PRESS

First published in 2008 by
CURRACH PRESS
55A Spruce Avenue, Stillorgan Industrial Park, Blackrock, Co. Dublin
www.currach.ie
1 3 5 4 2
Cover by Bluett
Origination by Currach Press
Printed in Ireland by ColourBooks, Baldoyle Industrial Estate, Dublin 13
ISBN: 978-1-85607-956-3

For Susan, Patrick and Claire

Contents

Preface

The idea for this book originated with the late Jim Kemmy TD in the autumn of 1997. I knew Jim from his work with the *Old Limerick Journal* and submitted an occasional article to the publication. Jim was very enthusiastic that this void in the history of Limerick should be filled. Sadly, Jim died unexpectedly, and my book on Donogh O'Malley was shelved for a number of years.

My interest in O'Malley was piqued again in recent years and with the encouragement and support of Currach publisher Jo O'Donoghue, the decision to write this book was made.

There are many gaps in this book, since the principal left few private documents, and his political career ended just as he was getting into his stride. The book is heavily reliant on the recollections of those who knew O'Malley. Each interview is unique but there are inevitable overlaps, which are compensated for by the originality and vivaciousness of the interviewees' memories and anecdotes.

A sincere thanks to all who contributed to this compilation:

Charlie Haughey invited me to Kinsaley: he was enthusiastic and wanted to make a contribution. However, I did not take the offer up at that time, and the tribunals, and later still, his poor health, precluded my interviewing him. A special thanks also to Seán Haughey TD.

Tom O'Donnell, former Fine Gael TD for Limerick East, Minister for the Gaeltacht, MEP and longtime family friend, was generous with his time, hospitality and interest. His admiration for Donogh, a member of the Opposition, transcends Party lines. That unity of purpose is gone, as is the old Limerick East constituency.

P.J. O'Donnell, the youngest of the O'Donnell brothers, offered keen insights into the mysteries and miracles of local politics. He is a fine orator and his political observations invariably turn to Edmund Burke.

Dr Dáithí Ó hÓgáin, Roinn an Bhéaloidis, UCD, has been supportive of this writer for many years. That he is a fellow Bruff native makes his inclusion here even more satisfying. '*Dáithí, a chara, go raibh míle…*'

Paddy Kiely from Pennywell in Limerick, an O'Malley man to the core, recalled his arguments, disagreements and making up with Donogh. O'Malley's death left Kiely with an enduring sadness and sense of loss.

Thanks to Clem Casey for verifying rugby queries.

Tony O'Dalaigh, who was O'Malley's private secretary, remembered a thoughtful, generous and mischievous minister.

The late Dr Peter Kavanagh, New York, a longtime acquaintance, was very helpful when in gregarious mood. His sharp mind and commentary on all things Irish are missed.

Michael Mills, political columnist and former ombudsman, wrote an important book, *Hurler on the Ditch*, and offered his memories and assistance, making himself available and answering phone queries. He was one of the few to observe the loneliness and apprehension of O'Malley in his final days.

Bruce Arnold also recognised that O'Malley may not have been a healthy man in the final months of his life.

Dr Paddy Hillery was gracious enough to take phone calls from me. He never got the credit for the foundation he put in place as Minister for Education, which allowed O'Malley to make his memorable declaration of free education.

Jack Bourke, raconteur, mischievous, penetrating and blunt in his account, always entertaining, ever the showman, enlivened many conversations with his wit and quick mind.

Tom English, a Fine Gael supporter but a great friend and admirer of Donogh O'Malley, goes back to a different time in Limerick city and county, a landscape changed out of all recognition. His account is tinged with nostalgia – and reasonably so.

Cormac Liddy spoke about the betrayal both of his father Rory and of Hilda O'Malley by a Fianna Fáil Party prompted by political expediency. It was a sad interlude that exposed the greed and self-serving nature of politics and politicians. A special thanks to Cormac for supplying many of the pictures in the book.

Senator Joe O'Toole met me in Leinster House and spoke about the Moriartys of Dingle.

Historian T. Ryle Dwyer and his mother Margaret offered relaxed hospitality and lively discussion in Tralee.

Desmond O'Malley, founder of the Progressive Democrats, 'the nephew', as he is referred to in Limerick (not the worst of the appendages) invited me to meet him in Dublin and was willing to detail his recollections.

Con Houlihan and I drank tea together and talked about the Moriartys and west Kerry. His assessment of Donogh O'Malley's contribution to the development of Irish society forms the basis of a chapter in this book.

Arthur Quinlan has had a varied career as a broadcaster, journalist and writer. Amateur golf is his passion and he can go on at length about the legendary players that he knew well and wrote about: Jimmy Bruen, Joe Carr, and nearer to our own time, a young Pádraig Harrington. He wrote a history of the renowned South Of Ireland Championship. The house that Quinlan lives in, Rocklawn, North Circular Road, Limerick, was designed and built by Donogh O'Malley in 1950. It was Quinlan who broke the news of Donogh's death to his son Daragh, and he shared some of his opinions and memories of Donogh with me.

Thanks to Father Tom Stack for recalling Donogh's final TV appearance, on Stack's *Outlook* programme on RTÉ.

Daragh O'Malley contributed key sections in this book. It is clear from his observations that he had the audaciousness and presence to make a fine politician but, having witnessed the insensitive treatment of his mother by the Fianna Fáil Party, he veered away from any political ambitions he might have had, choosing instead an acting career.

A special thanks to Vincent Browne for granting permission to draw on the John Healy profile of O'Malley from *Magill* magazine.

Thanks too to Aidan Corr, sports writer for the *Limerick Leader* and one of the most respected and insightful rugby writers in the country

A word of thanks to Michael Noonan, former Fianna Fáil TD, Meanus, County Limerick; to Tom Meany, neighbour, local historian, writer and raconteur – he hails from the oldest family in Bruff, with deep roots in Crawford's Lane;

and to Enda MacMahon of Harold's Cross, Dublin, for his exemplary research.

Finally, thanks to John, Kieran and Mr Bill and to my sisters Teresa Grufferty and Monica Kirwan.

PJ Browne, Bruff, February 2008

...to every task assigned to him. He lost no time in
showing his ca... when he was given his first

PROLOGUE

The day after Donogh O'Malley died, Monday 11 March 1968, the *Limerick Leader* paid tribute to him in a compelling and prescient editorial.

LIMERICK'S GREAT LOSS

The unexpected death of Mr Donogh O'Malley, TD, Minister for Education, at the early age of forty-seven years, has caused nationwide shock and grief. For his native city, however, this untimely end to a brilliant career comes as a blow from which the community will not recover for a very long time. Although Mr O'Malley was an outstanding politician and one of the most notable members of the Fianna Fáil Cabinet, he never forgot that he was first and foremost a Limerick man, and was unfailing in his efforts to promote the interests of the city and indeed of Limerick as a whole.

Limerick people well appreciated the vigour and forcefulness that the late minister brought to every task assigned to him. He lost no time in showing his calibre when he was given his first official appointment as Parliamentary Secretary to the Minister for Finance, with special charge to the Board of Works. One result of his push and drive was the speeding-up of many projects and the cutting through of much red tape. Later the same originality and dynamism was brought to bear in his task as Minister for Health. It was, however, as Minister for Education during the past three years that Mr O'Malley made his greatest contribution to the national wellbeing. The introduction of free post-primary education was a startling innovation. It allowed thousands of children to attend at secondary and vocational schools, who in their circumstances would be forced to end their education at national school level. It is not now but in the years to come that the country will reap the full benefits of this magnificent step forward. Again the Minister took a revolutionary step in deciding to proceed with a rationalisation scheme for university education. Although it may take some time to bring this into being, it is now part and parcel of the policy of the government, and the groundwork has been laid for its implementation in due course.

Mr O'Malley had a boundless capacity for work. He drove himself hard, and he expected the same enthusiasm from those who served under him in the various departments. He has been described as a man in a hurry, and certainly one of the traits which made a secure place for him on the national scene was his impatience of everything that he regarded would lead to delay in progress. He could at times be testy, and he was a formidable political opponent, but he had the facility for gaining friends on all sides. Indeed the deceased minister can, without exaggeration, be described as one of the most popular members of the Dáil. He gained a reputation for courtesy and patience in dealing with members of the Opposition Party, and these traits were very well appreciated, more especially since they are not too readily apparent in some of the other young ministers.

Nearer home, Mr O'Malley never lost contact with the people, and it did not matter what political views one held, he was invariably willing to be of assistance when called upon. The queue of people outside his office each Saturday morning testified to his accessibility, and the thoroughness with which he pursued his chosen career. It can now be said in retrospect that the minister overworked himself in the cause of the nation and the people of Limerick. His political career was not without personal disappointments and inevitable frustration. These, however, are inevitable in public life, where blame and praise are equally to be expected. Mr O'Malley strove mightily for Limerick and one of his greatest worries of recent times has been the high unemployment figures.

This sad tragedy has cost Limerick its greatest protagonist. At the moment it is impossible to

discern anybody on the horizon of the calibre
that goes to make a successful minister of state.
We can only mourn an outstanding son of
Limerick, while offering profound sympathy to
Mrs O'Malley and the members of the family.

Donogh O'Malley poses a challenge for biographers and
researchers alike because his private papers are practically
non-existent. The researcher is denied the illumination of
critical primary source material. Furthermore, since O'Malley
died at the age of forty-seven, his career in politics was
attenuated. Even so, there is no shortage of memoirs of the
1960s' generation, considerable statistical studies and Dáil
debates. More important than any of these is the enquiring
mind, that enables one to reflect on the transformation of
Ireland in the last four decades of the twentieth century.

The defining point of Donogh O'Malley's political career
was the introduction of free secondary education. Sadly, his
death is associated with the insensitivity, ruthlessness and
self–promotion involved in filling his vacant Dáil seat. Hilda
O'Malley, devastated by the loss of her husband, declined the
initial overtures to contest the seat. This paved the way for
Des O'Malley to enter the political arena and take it.

Rory Liddy, Donogh's close friend and founder of the
Fianna Fáil parliamentary Party in Limerick, was never
considered, although he was Donogh's choice for the seat.
'The seat is yours Rory, take it,' were O'Malley's last words
to him after he suffered his first heart attack on 10 March
1968.

Liddy quickly learned of the change in attitude among
Fianna Fáil activists, and he wasn't considered as a replacement

for Donogh. This episode reflected poorly on Fianna Fáil in Limerick, leaving the Party fractured.

Hilda was deserving of a seat in Seanad Éireann, but found herself instead finishing her internship in order to practise medicine. Rory Liddy was airbrushed out and was left with nothing. He had good reason to be embittered but, ever a man of integrity, he drifted away in dignified silence.

1

'THE SCOURGE OF THE MILL ROAD'

Donogh Brendan O'Malley was born on 18 January 1921, into a well-off Limerick professional family. His path through life was already delineated as one of privilege and social advancement. That's not to say that the family was extravagant, but there was the comfort and assurance that their status conferred on them. Their social status was inaccessible to the majority of working class or unemployed people in the city.

In September of that year, Limerick won the All-Ireland Hurling Championship. The new Football Association of Ireland (FAI) was founded in Dublin after a split from the Belfast-based Irish Football Association.

On a more sombre note, violence and destruction were rampant in the city. The new year saw an escalation of the violence as the Troubles reached a peak, followed by the inexorable onset of the Civil War.

Fighting broke out in Limerick early in July 1922, following the fatal shooting of a Free State soldier; Private Thomas O'Brien of Upper William Street, in Parnell Street (then known as Nelson Street), by a Republican patrol. The battle for control of the city was waged for almost ten days.

Hundreds of people from the centre of the city fled to the sanctuary of Mungret College, where the Jesuit priests ran a temporary centre for refugees. There was widespread destruction as each street was fought for: the Strand Barracks were shelled; the Castle Barracks, close to King John's Castle, were captured from the Republican forces who had been in occupation. The Republican forces were obliged to evacuate the city. Later figures revealed that eight Free State troops were killed, and between twenty and thirty Republicans.

The O'Malleys were staunch supporters of Cumann na nGaedheal. Like many of their class, they wanted to see an end to hostilities and a return to stability. The restoration of law and order would have been uppermost in their minds, even though they were well removed from the looting and destruction in the city.

The O'Malleys lived on the Mill Road in Corbally, an upper-class stronghold, home to the city's major businessmen. Built on high ground, these quintessential 19th-century houses overlooked the magnificent vistas of the Shannon and Abbey rivers. High walls were used to screen them from the road even though the precincts were still not built on. Only two cars used the road on a regular basis, one belonging to Joseph O'Malley, the other belonging to a Matt Russell

Most of the houses were built before 1856, including Corbally House, Riverview, Willowbank Cottage, Roseneath Cottage, Prospect Villa, Prospect House and Geraldine Cottage. In later years new owners dropped the word cottage, uncomfortable with its lowly connotation.

Riverview is generally regarded as being the finest house on the Mill Road. It was there that Donogh, one of a family of ten children, was born and spent his formative years. Donogh and his three brothers and six sisters were christened in St Patrick's, then parish church for Corbally.

The house was purchased in 1903 by Donogh's father, Joseph O'Malley, who was an assistant county surveyor. He had previously lived at Willowbank, at the end of the Mill Road. After the death of his first wife, he remarried. Mary, his new bride, was uncomfortable with the island situation of that house and the presence of rats in the river.

Joseph O'Malley died in 1933, when Donogh was twelve, and Mary sold the house to Charles O'Malley, a dentist. Desmond O'Malley, Donogh's brother, bought it back in 1942 when he was Mayor of Limerick.

Father Tom Stack grew up on O'Connell Avenue close to where Donogh O'Malley's mother lived. The families would have known each other as neighbours, and the O'Malley and Stack mothers were on friendly terms. Stack was too young to have known Donogh very well, but he does remember O'Malley coming home on break from University in Galway.

'I have a distinct memory of Donogh coming home one Christmas and we had a lot of snow. That was when we used to get good snowfalls. All the youngsters in the area were out throwing snowballs. "I'll show ye how to make good ones," he told us, and sure enough he gathered the snow in his hands and shaped it into a firm round missile. "These ones will hurt them," he explained to us as he made several more. He was a bit of a mischievous rogue in that way. He always had that sense of play about him, a likeable spontaneity.

Denis O'Shaughnessy describes some of Donogh's youthful misdemeanours in *How's Your Father? Stories Of Limerick* (1992):

'One fine summer's morning many years ago, Mrs Mary Loughran of the Mill Road in Corbally answered her door to a neighbouring young lad by the name of Donogh O'Malley. After a few pleasantries were exchanged young Donogh offered her a compact of face powder at a very reasonable price and in a time of great scarcity. She asked no questions and was glad to purchase it.

'That Saturday afternoon she walked into town. It was a warm summer's day and by the time she reached O'Connell Street she had perspired somewhat. She noticed that people were looking strangely at her. Eventually an acquaintance stopped her and said: 'Oh Mary, what has happened to your face?'

'Her friend produced a mirror from her purse and Mrs Loughran died a thousand deaths as she beheld her face all streaked and with several white patches showing through.

'She had been duped by the bould Donogh. Desperately short of funds, he had taken one of his sister's half-filled boxes and mixed the powder with flour to fill it up, with disastrous results for poor Mrs Loughran!

'The Scourge of the Mill Road, who was to go on to become one of the nation's best-known politicians and innovative Cabinet minister, had struck again!

'Another day, a neighbour, John McInerney of Ard na Gréine, answered a knock at the door to an attractive young girl.

'"I'm here from the agency regarding the domestic you were looking for," she said to the bemused customs official.

'"I'm afraid you have the wrong house, young lady. As far as I know Mrs McInerney isn't looking for a maid."

'"But it said on the advertisement that you were," said the girl, and she began to cry.

'At this stage John didn't quite know what to do and was mightily relieved when into the drive cycled Mrs McInerney after her trip to town.

'She twigged straight away that this was no young domestic but her young neighbour Donogh O'Malley, dressed in one of his sister's frocks. He quickly melted into the shrubbery when he realised the game was up.

'Mrs McInerney prided herself on her apple tarts. When they were cooked she would put them on the windowsill to cool off, as was the custom of the time. She noticed that tarts began to go missing and wasn't quite sure whether the dog was the culprit or not. Keeping watch one day she saw a hand creeping over the sill and she caught hold of it, exposing the culprit as, you needn't guess, the future mayor of the city.

'Close neighbours living in the double lodge leading to the O'Malley residence Riverview, and Alma Fitt's house Mary Villa, were at one stage not on the best of terms. This state of affairs was exacerbated when one morning the wives found that one another's washing had been switched from their respective lines and another scene ensued. If they had looked up at the window of Riverview they would have seen the innocent-looking face of a young Donogh, beside himself with laughter.

'Laughter turned to tears on another occasion when as a young boy, Donogh was disciplined for some misdemeanour when his father barred him from a pleasure trip in the family car, one of only two in use in the Mill Road at the time. When his parents returned that night he waited until they were about to enter the front door and then poured a bucket of water down on them from a bedroom window. It is not recorded what the retributions were.

'Donogh and his brothers Desmond and Michael all in their turn uniquely held the distinguished office of Mayor of Limerick. Desmond was a strong supporter of Duffy's Blueshirts but in an arena of high political tension was concerned that, on his way to rallies in town, his uniform would attract unwarranted attention. He eventually got the use of a room in Geary's Hotel in Thomas Street which he used for changing into the blue shirt.

'Donogh's father Joseph, who was Assistant County Surveyor, had loyalist tendencies and on royal occasions during the Occupancy years, the Union Jack could be seen fluttering from the roof of Riverview. Some years after the Treaty, Joseph's wife was selling poppies in town on Armistice day and was approached by Seán Carroll, an IRA activist from Castleconnell, who told her to desist, which she wisely did.

'Mr and Mrs McInerney were Fianna Fáil supporters and on one occasion when Mrs McInerney was cycling in her drive, young Donogh jumped out of the bushes waving the Union Jack, exclaiming: 'Ye'll get yeer bellyful of the Long Fella [de Valera] yet.'

'Little did the McInerneys or Donogh himself realise at the time that when he entered the political arena, he would drift from the family's traditional Blueshirt stance to Fianna Fáil, and that Dev himself would become one of his mentors.'

School and University

Donogh received a typical middle-class education at two Jesuit schools, the Crescent at Limerick and Clongowes Wood in County Kildare. Later he would attend University College Galway and complete a degree in Civil Engineering. He grew up in Ireland's third largest city – the three main features, the River Shannon, St Mary's Cathedral and King John's Castle retained their pre-eminence although they were later surrounded by many other buildings and embellishments.

'Limerick was more Roman Catholic that the Vatican,' wrote Terry Wogan. 'Not a lot of Christianity, if by that you mean love and tolerance of your fellow man, but plenty of religion.'

In the 1930s and 1940s, Ireland became a closed, introspective society, with relentless banning of books and films as the rigid censorship laws were applied. In Limerick the climate of oppression was even more pronounced, largely because of the powerful influence of the Redemptorists Arch-Confraternity among the working class. The Church cultivated the wealthier classes, and membership of the Arch-Confraternity provided an opportunity to become pillars of local society through the church.

O'Malley was well suited to the Jesuit regime at the Crescent. The school was renowned for learning, scholarship and discipline. O'Malley was quick-minded and bright. He was also an outstanding rugby player for the college and was allowed a latitude not enjoyed by others. He was rarely in trouble with the Jesuits and when caught for some devilment or prank he invariably bluffed his way out of it. Even as a young teenager there was a precocious presence about him.

After finishing at the Crescent, he spent a year at Clongowes Wood in County Kildare, where his rugby ability was noted. He was also involved in drama and debating and, overall, acquitted himself with distinction. He was tall, well built and self-assured. He was well liked and made friends easily. Fellow-students gravitated toward him; life was rarely dull when O'Malley was around.

O'Malley's star continued to rise after he enrolled in University College Galway to study civil engineering. His rugby career began in earnest during these years in Galway. His sporting talent, combined with an impressive level of fitness, saw him win inter-provincial honours for Connacht. He would go on to represent Munster and Ulster. He was a competitive swimmer from his days at the Blue Star Swimming Club in Limerick.

College life opened up a new social dimension for him and it was probably during these years that he started to drink. He was young, and his capacity for drink matched his appetite for it. For the most part his drinking was based around social events, post-match sessions and dances. After he graduated from UCG his tendency to binge-drink became manifest.

It was around this time that he became acquainted with Audrey Harris, the elder sister of Richard Harris. The Harris family was well to do and ran a flour and milling business in Limerick. During these years, the business was thriving, and Donogh and Audrey would meet at the Harris home in Overdale. The young couple fell in love and were engaged to be married. Their courtship was romantic and gallant.

Richard Harris used to tell a story about those times. One night as he lay in bed, he heard a voice coming up from the street in the direction of Audrey's window. It was Donogh, serenading her at about two in the morning with: 'She Was the Miller's Daughter Fair.'

It was not to be, however. Audrey fell ill with a stomach complaint that was diagnosed as intestinal cancer. Repeated operations and therapy were unsuccessful and she was sent home to Overdale, where she died in February 1946 at the age of twenty-one. Her engagement ring was buried with her.

It was a devastating setback for O'Malley, who was then twenty-five. The O'Malley and Harris families remained close.

The war years cut short Donogh's promising rugby career, as no international fixtures could be played. He had the talent and the desire to make it as an international for Ireland. Now his rugby career was essentially over and he had lost the woman he was due to marry.

2

Donogh and Hilda…and Patrick Kavanagh

'I saw the danger, yet I walked along the enchanted
way,'
Patrick Kavanagh, 'On Raglan Road'

In 1946, the same year as the death of Audrey Harris, Donogh
O'Malley met Hilda Moriarty. Hilda was born in Dingle in
1922. She had aspirations to be a writer, but when she was
sixteen, her father, who was a doctor, brought her to Dublin
and enrolled her in the medical school at UCD. One of her
classmates at the time was Paddy Hillery.

According their his son Daragh, 'Donogh met Hilda
Moriarty for the first time at a rugby match in Tralee. He was
playing with Shannon, and he spotted Hilda watching from
the sidelines. After the match he asked the Kerry lads who
she was. When he got back to Limerick, he sat down and
wrote her an eight-page letter in green Biro, and they later
met in Dublin.

Donogh and Hilda married in Adare in August 1947.
They set up home at 29 Lanarone Avenue, Corbally, which
was around the corner from the Mill Road and the house
Donogh grew up in, Riverview.

'My mother was very supportive of Donogh's political

career,' says Daragh O'Malley. She was a fluent Irish speaker, and although she didn't try to influence us to speak the language, she would often express herself in Irish. She once told me that she thought in Irish but of course that wasn't very practical. She spoke Irish to my father to give him a working knowledge of the language, and any speeches he had to make in Irish were always polished by her.

'I never did find out why my mother didn't practise medicine until after my father died. She was a qualified doctor when she married my father, in 1947, and my sister Suzanne wasn't born until 1952. That was quite a long gap, but it was possibly a Moriarty trait. My mother's sister, Dorothy O'Neill, was also a qualified doctor who never practised. There were various other Moriarty relatives who were qualified in medicine but who never wrote a prescription. Then there was Hilda's brother, Cyril Moriarty; he was a pilot in the Royal Air Force and saw active service in Aden.

'The Moriartys might well be described as a peculiar if distinctive family and this applied to cousins and distant relatives as well. Father Tom Moriarty for instance, parish priest of Ballyferriter, was a very colourful and erudite man and a great friend of the actor Barry Fitzgerald. He wrote letters every week to my mother. They were very close. Tom was a leading apprentice jockey before joining the clergy, and he lived to a great age.'

Fellow-Kerryman Con Houlihan knew Hilda's father, Paddy Moriarty, by repute: 'Paddy Moriarty was many years a practitioner in west Kerry. He was famous for two things; he was a good doctor and he was a brave man. There were nights when he'd have to go out to the Blasket Islands or Valentia, and the stormy sea wouldn't worry him. He was courageous, loyal and caring. He tended all with kindness, rich and poor alike, and he charged little or he charged nothing. If you had no money you'd offer him a goose or a turkey; more often than not he wouldn't take it. I'm telling you he was a God and a saint in west Kerry. Hilda was the same way up in Limerick after her husband died and she finished her medical studies. No one was ever turned away and she wanted little or no money.

'When Hilda came to college in Dublin she was a very beautiful girl. She associated with another beautiful girl, Kathleen Ryan. When Hilda and Kathleen were seen together walking down Grafton Street, they were quite a sight. Your heart would jump up. Kathleen's brother John Ryan owned the Bailey and patronised the literary scene.

Kathleen was a reluctant film star. She took part in one fairly good film, *Odd Man Out*, and one great film, *Esther Waters,* based on the book by George Moore, which was set in the English racing world of the late nineteenth century. Kathleen was brilliant in that.

'Hilda went her own way of course, and I last met her at the Irish Cup coursing meeting in Clounanna around 1977. She was in the company of a well known GAA and coursing reporter.

'Hilda had a big influence on her husband. He came from a better-off class in Limerick and she was a doctor's daughter. Hilda knew how poor west Kerry was in her time. And I can tell you it was poor. I'll give you an example and you might laugh at this. There was a programme on over Christmas recorded back in Dunquin, very far west Kerry. There were seven women who'd be my age, and they were talking about the presents they for got for Christmas when they were thirteen or fourteen.

'One woman said: "Now Mary, Pat, Peig, I'll tell ye one thing. When I woke Christmas morning and found an orange in my stocking I was happy beyond belief." Sure you'd take an orange for granted today, but that tells you how poor west Kerry was. The west of Ireland was basically poverty-stricken. If the fishing wasn't good there was nothing there...nothing, boy. The tourists came latterly but before that people merely existed.

'What they did have, though, was great courage and great spirit; it kept them going. And another thing they had was mental cooperation, a spiritual dimension that's probably gone now. In my time in Kerry there was a great spirit of community. In west Kerry they had an old saying – people living in each others' shadows. [*Ar scáth a chéile a mhaireas na daoine.*] That's gone, as are a lot of things. Comparative prosperity took it away; everybody has a car now.

'Long ago every parish had its own field and you played something there after work. The boys played hurling or football and the women came and talked about hens or recipes for making jam. The field was a social focus. West Kerry has prospered through tourism – I suppose it makes money for some, but life is still hard there and heavily reliant on fishing. I wouldn't say that west Kerry is a paradise. I don't fairly well know. The west of the country generally has it tough because the movement is towards the east.

Hilda was a friend to the poor in Limerick. Ask the people down there. I know this to be true from my rugby friends around Young Munster and the Parish. In her own way she was a counterpart of her husband. Donogh's contribution was on a national scale, the whole country benefited. Hilda, in her own way, carried on locally what Donogh had started nationally.

'Their son Daragh O'Malley is a very fine person and a great actor. He's a friend of mine and was often here in the house. The O'Malley name in Limerick will forever be held in great esteem. It will be similarly revered in west Kerry.'

'MORE PROSAIC THAN POETIC'

Patrick Kavanagh wrote in the *Standard* of 28 March 1947:

> Romantic love is not quite the fortuitous happening
> it is made out to be. There is a considerable element
> of will about falling in love. There is more of a
> suicide than an accidental death about it.

It's intriguing that an inconsequential friendship should continue to resonate so enduringly in the mythology of modern Irish poetry. Patrick Kavanagh and Hilda Moriarty were not lovers. Their relationship (such as it was) has been tailored and exaggerated to suit various points of view. The truth is more prosaic.

As Kavanagh indicated, love is an act of will. It is useless to seek perfection in someone else. To love someone is to see all the faults and love anyway. In the end, this is the way to accept oneself. Hilda Moriarty was not impressed by Kavanagh or his poetry. She would have known many a similar character around Dingle.

Kavanagh's persistence in befriending her and pursuing her is the stuff of popular legend. Though not malicious or hurtful to those involved the story enables us to perpetuate a myth we find comforting. Hilda was intelligent and blessed with that insouciant west Kerry pragmatism. That she strung Kavanagh along until she found a better suitor is fiction.

She was fond of the poet, but no more than that. She never felt sorry for him and was disappointed that he was drifting along in life hoping for an opportunity that he felt was rightfully his. That's not how life was lived in west Kerry, and Hilda's compassion was withdrawn when she saw through this.

Patrick Hillery, who preceded Donogh O'Malley as Minister for Education, knew Hilda when they were both at UCD:

'She was in the same class as me in medical school. She was a very beautiful looking girl, and before you ask, I was already seeing a girl at the time! Hilda was well got, one of the Moriartys from Dingle. They were a great family and her father was legendary in the way he looked after his patients.

'The association with Kavanagh has been well documented I'd say. But he wasn't Hilda's type at all. He was kind of slovenly and maybe that was the best he could do but Paddy Moriarty wouldn't have wanted his daughter hanging around with the likes of him. I used to see him around Dublin when I was a student, but I never had anything to do with him.

The inspiration for 'On Raglan Road' was hardly romantic. She met the poet one evening in Dublin by accident, to learn that he was unemployed and on the touch. He had been having a difficulty writing, he added. She suggested that he write something more marketable and move away from the bogs and the cattle and sheep of rural Monaghan. Write about people, she told him, something interesting. She continued to challenge him to do this and he finally relented and said he would write a poem about a woman. 'Of course I can write a poem about a woman. In fact I'll write a poem about you, Hilda. I'll immortalise you in poetry.'

Kavanagh was as good as his word, but even he could not have predicted the enduring popularity of this song, especially in versions by Luke Kelly and Sinéad O'Connor.

Peter Kavanagh, a formidable if contentious intellect, was the defiant keeper of his brother's flame, accumulating an impressive body of source material that might otherwise have been lost. According to him:

> Patrick's association with Hilda came to naught,
> as might be expected…Just the same, the romance
> could not be called a failure. He got several good
> poems out of the misery.

Kavanagh got a lot more than that from the O'Malleys. Donogh was fond of him and gave him a few quid whenever they met. Hilda used to tell her husband: 'You must do something about Kavanagh. Tell Haughey to give him a few pounds.' John A. Costello was good to Kavanagh after humiliating him in the libel case in 1954. Kavanagh said he voted for him anyway; he said the same thing to Fianna Fáil.

Kavanagh never stopped writing to Hilda, even when her children were born and growing.

'It was probably a country thing with him,' says Daragh. 'Every so often Kavanagh would send a telegram to Sunville addressed to Dr Hilda O'Malley. The telegram usually had a tip for a horse in an upcoming big race.

'One time his tip hit the jackpot. This was in 1961 when he tipped Nicolaus Silver to win the Grand National. The horse, trained by Fred Rimell and ridden by Bobby Beasley, came in at 28/1 and I think my mother had three quid each way on him. With the winnings she bought a grand piano which was thereafter known as Kavanagh's Grand Piano. It was Kavanagh who got Hilda interested in the horses when they were friends in Dublin – Kavanagh was always doing doubles and trebles at the betting shop in Duke Street, next to the Bailey and in later life, Hilda loved nothing more than placing a weekly bet in McWilliams's betting shop in Henry Street in Limerick

'When Kavanagh died in 1967, both my parents were saddened. Hilda did say that Paddy never fully recovered from lung surgery. She sent a wreath to the funeral. I read somewhere that this gesture was a token of her undying love for him. That's absolute rubbish! It reminds me of one of Kavanagh's great lines – "Gods make their own importance".'

'ENDURING FIDELITY'
In her biography of Patrick Kavanagh, Antoinette Quinn writes of Donogh O'Malley: 'His courtship of Hilda was lavish and spectacular. He travelled from Limerick to take her for romantic dinners in Dublin and showered her with expensive gifts.' There is no basis for this observation; O'Malley was not particularly well-to-do at this point in his life. Handsome, yes, charismatic, yes, but not affluent enough for the kind of courtship alluded to.

Quinn's account of the O'Malley/Moriarty/Kavanagh triad is a bewildering section of this biography. O'Malley was not the least bit threatened by the older Kavanagh and found his occasional company on their dates amusing. He never looked upon Kavanagh as a rival; he felt compassion for the older man and if he had money he'd slip him a few pounds.

Kavanagh made the most of the so-called letdown by the younger woman, and this is where confusion arose later on. To write that he was tortured, distraught and even heartbroken is an exaggeration. Quinn underestimates the cunning and durability of the peasant mentality that Kavanagh had in abundance. His brother Peter said:

> Patrick was under no illusions about Hilda. He was out of his depth there and he knew it; we all knew it. He had plenty of women available to him for various needs and he was happy to play the role of the jilted, crestfallen lover. He became a big admirer of O'Malley in later years.

There is no evidence for Quinn's claim that Kavanagh acquired a painting of Hilda and kept it in his room at 62 Pembroke Road for years, 'propped against a wall, an image of his enduring fidelity'.

Most confusing of all is Quinn's characterisation of Hilda's marriage:

> Hilda's marriage was not an altogether happy one for, while he sought her advice in political matters and trusted her to write or fine-tune his speeches, Donogh was a ladies' man who persistently and publicly sought the company of other women. Hilda for her part never quite lost her interest in Kavanagh, although they apparently didn't see one another again until the last months of his life.

According to Tony O'Dalaigh, who was Donogh O'Malley's private secretary in the Department of Education, O'Malley's reputation as a womaniser has no basis outside of gossip-writers and mischief-makers. After giving up the drink he was even more unlikely to stray.

'I would see Hilda from time to time. Certain events, major functions, she would have to attend. You can divide politicians' wives into two – those who want to be up there, in the news, being photographed, and those who don't. Hilda, I thought, was shy. She would attend but was quite happy to remain in the background, very self-assured and dignified. She was not the Chérie Blair or Hillary Clinton type and was content to live in Limerick with the children.

'If Donogh was involved with any women,' says O'Dalaigh, 'he certainly kept it very close to himself. The drivers would know about these things, and we had no evidence in the office. He'd never say to me, "I had a great night with a bird last night." There is no doubt that women were attracted to him. He had a big fan club.

'Moreover, Hilda O'Malley was one of the most beautiful women in the country. She had great presence; indeed she had been called to Hollywood for a screen test with a view to starring in a film but she lost out to Maureen O'Hara.' Invariably, truth is supplanted by myth in deference to tabloid money.

When Kavanagh died Hilda did send a wreath of red roses arranged in the form of an 'H'. 'This posthumous love token,' Quinn writes, 'acknowledges that the affair had not been altogether one-sided. He was the frog prince of a young woman's fairytale who, alas, had never metamorphosed into a marriageable partner.'

Joe O'Toole has a sense of Hilda Moriarty being a quint-essential west Kerry woman: matriarchal, pragmatic, not likely to defer to the likes of an O'Malley or any man. 'When I first came to Dublin,' says O'Toole, 'I found the women's liberation movement bewildering, to say the least. My formative years were spent in Dingle, a town where businesses were dominated by women. There was no doubt about who was in charge, and who made the important decisions. Hilda would have had those imposing traits as well.'

Father Tom Stack, himself the author of a book on Patrick Kavanagh (*No Earthly Estate: God and Patrick Kavanagh*, 2002), says that Donogh was not in the slightest bit threatened by Kavanagh: 'He was very fond of Kavanagh and would give him a few pounds every time they met. Kavanagh was alert to this of course and would sometimes show up at a function when he knew Donogh might be there. Shortly after he was made Minister for Health, Donogh was the principal speaker at a medical conference in Dublin. It would have been well publicised and Kavanagh got wind of it so off he went. He was a bit the worse for wear from the drink. As I remember it, the building was very warm; the heating was working too well.

'The combination of heat and drink was too much for Kavanagh and he fainted, or appeared to faint. There was a bit of a panic and the meeting was interrupted. Next thing I hear Donogh shouting "Will someone effin' do something for Kavanagh." It was more comical than life-threatening and I think Kavanagh was able to get up and walk away, no doubt with a few quid in his pocket.'

Political journalist and author Bruce Arnold was also acquainted with Patrick Kavanagh: 'I knew him. We lived in Wilford Place and he used to frequent Baggot Street Bridge. He wasn't an easy man to know, but he was much more of a gentleman than people thought, and he was a lot more educated than he was given credit for.'

Bruce Arnold was never timid about voicing his convictions: 'He deserved the Nobel Prize for his poetry, but he blotted his copybook in other ways and didn't get it.'

3

'Off His Head on the Drink'

O'Malley's reputation for the drink preceded him to Dáil Éireann. He was very approachable; he would talk to the well-heeled, the poor, the down and outs, and was generous with his money. He was welcome in all sporting hostelries in Limerick, even when he got into brawls and broke up the place. That would a badge of honour for the pubs in question. He paid immediately for the damages and in a relatively small city he wasn't hard to locate.

Cruises Hotel was the mecca in those days. After-hours drinking was allowed in the private bar at the Limerick Boat Club. The main entrance was padlocked, which made it more difficult for the local Gardaí to gain entry.

When 'he was off his head on the drink', taxi drivers would avoid him. The line between exuberance and violence was often blurred. He was quick-fisted and could handle himself in a barroom brawl. One could write a small book on his escapades, and the stories about the stories. There is no disputing that, at times, he was very violent when drunk.

Clem Casey, synonymous in Limerick with Young Munster Rugby Club, and Mayor of the City in 1980, was friendly with O'Malley. Casey lived over the family shop in Roche's Street. When not selling poultry in the shop and supplying the local hospitals with potatoes, he was devoted to his twin passions of rugby and politics.

'I was very fond of him. He was chalk and cheese to Dessie. Every week you got a letter from Donogh and you gave that into the *Leader* office and you'd get a news item: "Clem Casey has been informed by the Minister that the tarmacadam would be put down in the next month." He was great in that regard and very fond of the councillors.

'We went to the races one day and Donogh was there dressed to kill. He had a tip for a horse named Treaty Stone. We all backed the horse and Donogh was watching the race using binoculars. When asked how the horse was doing, he handed the binoculars to Vincent Feeney, saying, "The fuckin' horse must have the Treaty Stone tied on to his balls."

'There was a man who went to Donogh to get his son into the guards. He didn't get in and the father went back to Donogh giving out yards. Donogh explained that the young man had had a row with the guards in the past. "What about it. Didn't you have rows with the guards yourself?" said the father. "I did, but I never tried to join them," said Donogh.'

Daragh O'Malley says that Donogh's excessive drinking was 'well known to Seán Lemass and Éamon De Valera; as many of his so-called escapades were quickly brought to their attention. His ascension in the Party would have been feared by several of his rivals and there would be a certain amount of begrudgery going on all the time. His begrudgers in the Party would have felt that as long as my father was drinking, or rumoured to be drinking, their positions in Cabinet were safe.

'One of the reasons my father drank was because of his

frustration at being passed over for promotion in the Party. He was a TD for ten years and he saw others who had entered the Dáil with him making their way up the political ladder, people who were clearly no more capable than he was.

'Of course no single factor brings about alcoholism. We have a tendency to advance simplistic solutions for complex problems. The thinking now is that it is due to many factors which can vary from individual to individual.

'Donogh's mother didn't approve of his drinking. She felt that not only was he associating with the wrong crowd in Limerick, but that he would never amount to much if he continued that lifestyle. She expressed a desire for him to move abroad; she was concerned that he might bring shame and scandal on the family in Limerick.

'Hilda, on the other hand, had a more pragmatic attitude when it came to the drink. She wasn't happy about the way he drank and the late nights. The call would come in from a porter in Cruises or some other hostelry, announcing that Donogh was comatose again, and asking her to come immediately and take him home. Off she'd go in her blue Morris Minor at two or three in the morning and get him. My father didn't simply get drunk; he would drink himself into a stupor and fall asleep.

'My mother had her own intuition about drink. She would have seen plenty of drinking in her own family in west Kerry and this tempered her attitude. After my father's death she studied psychiatry in Ipswich, and later specialised in the treatment of alcoholism. She was renowned for her helpful attitude towards alcoholics and their families. She never regarded alcoholism as a disease; to her it was a human failing, the refuge of the inadequate or an escape from the stresses of life. Of course my father was profuse in his apologies after he sobered up, and wrote her letters vowing that this was the last time, that he was swearing off the drink for good.'

The Bust of G. K. Chesterton

According to Daragh O'Malley, the 'door' incident has been well chronicled and there are several versions depending on the source.

'Donogh was in the Dáil bar drinking when the bell rang for all deputies to attend the chamber for a vote. An usher in the Dáil at the time alerted my father. Donogh was seconds late for the vote and the doors were automatically closed. He started kicking and banging his fists on the great door, roaring, "Let me in, Let me in!"

'There was a bronze bust of G.K. Chesterton, the poet, outside the entrance to the Dáil chamber. Donogh got hold of the bust and in frustration fired it at the door, causing the door to crack. That incident received national publicity and was the last straw for Fianna Fáil Party brass. Donogh was sent to see de Valera to explain his actions.

'In the meantime, Opposition and even a few Fianna Fáil deputies were calling for severe punishment. Whether or not this was a wake-up call for my father to curb his drinking is hard to say. De Valera was sympathetic, and I think Lemass had a genuine fondness for him.

Donogh explained that he wanted to be able to do more for Limerick and he could only do this if he was given a worthwhile position in the Cabinet. He added that he found his situation very frustrating and that made it very difficult for him to get any meaningful work done. In any case, he convinced them that if he was given a chance by way of a Cabinet position he would stay off the drink Lemass succumbed to his charm but insisted that this was his very last chance.

'Donogh joined the AA and, except for going on the odd unnoticed batter, stayed off the drink and went on to what was to become a very productive phase of his political career.. He was happy that he was no longer going to be left behind. Now he had a real opportunity to do something substantial for the poor of Limerick.'

4

Sunville Days

It's a rare day that Daragh O'Malley doesn't remember the Limerick of his childhood, the city and environs where he was born and reared. Myriad images take him back daily to this landscape of the mind – to the Markets Field, Thomond Park, Wembley Rovers, Kilkee every summer, and of course the Lyric, the Savoy, the Grand Central, the Royal and the Carlton cinemas. Born out Corbally way, he remembers the years in Sunville, near the heart of the city, the home to which the O'Malley family moved from Corbally. He remembers the apple trees, the carefully manicured gardens, serving Mass every morning at the Salesian Convent, and walks along Barrington's Piers which led on to the Shannon. During those years the city merged directly and quickly with an unhurried countryside.

Daragh and his sister Suzanne grew up in a lively home, frequented by politicians and statesmen. They were indulged and sustained by loving parents, Donogh O'Malley, a true son of Limerick, and west-Kerry native Hilda Moriarty. Daragh recalls a near-idyllic existence, where opinions were expressed freely at meals and punctuated by laughter and mischief. 'I had a very happy childhood,' he says.

'I put on plays in a huge garage; Paddy Hough, a wizard

48

carpenter, was commissioned by my mother to build a stage and for years all and sundry came to see shows such as *Jack and the Beanstalk* and *Francis of Assisi*. Richard Leonard, now a high-flying Limerick accountant, always seemed to get the lead in our plays – I really can't think why! Our acting troupe was called the Sunville Players.

'I played a lot of rugby for Crescent College but, much to the chagrin of the Jesuits, I loved playing soccer with Wembley Rovers and eventually formed my own team, Northend United. I also printed a weekly newspaper called *The Sunville Times*. I had two dogs, a cat named Topsy, a budgie called Budgie and twenty-two rabbits.' A busy childhood indeed!

Like his father, Daragh is opinionated, strong-willed and vocal. Unlike Donogh, who was always nervous before going on television or giving a speech, the son is at ease in any media setting, performing easily for a live audience, with a gift for mimicry and storytelling:

'My father was a qualified engineer, and he set up practice in O'Connell Street, over the Whitehouse Pub. He did various design jobs around Limerick and one of his first jobs was the City Theatre and the Lyric Cinema in the city. He then started a company which he called St James's Park Housing Society; my father had a fancy for all things relating to the court of St James. He built St James's Park on the Ennis Road in partnership with Limerick builder Robert Parks. In naming another housing scheme that he built he reverted to the line "I dreamt of green fields," from Shakespeare's *Henry V*, so he called it Greenfields. Donogh also built Patrick's Road and Rosbrien.

'He got a few quid from the building and bought Sunville

House from the Cleeve family, a name synonymous with toffee manufacture. One of the Cleeve sons was the well-known author and broadcaster, Brian.

'Donogh paid £6,200 for Sunville House, which was an enormous price in those days. It was an eighteen-bedroom mansion with a ballroom and a games room and set out on twenty-seven acres. My father didn't initially think we'd live in the house because its size and upkeep were astronomical, but we moved in anyway. We had a nanny, Nana Croke, a housekeeper called Mrs Shinnors, and there were Mr Coster the gardener, and Paddy the handyman.

'Later on, Donogh turned half the house into apartments and, in partnership with Robert Parks, developed the land and restored the remaining orchards to their former glory. It became known as the Sunville Estate, which indeed it was. Think about the incongruity in all of this – a local TD, a man who felt more at home with the poor of Limerick, living in such splendour and grandeur. In any case it did him no harm locally since he was the same old 'Dunnick' to every decent constituent and chancer in the city.

'Donogh became increasingly involved in the building sector in Limerick and was quite successful. He bought the Brazen Head pub in O'Connell Street and refurbished it, spending £100,000, an astonishing sum at the time, and creating an upscale restaurant the likes of which Limerick had never seen. The legendary architect Sam Stephenson was commissioned to design the premises.

'Not surprisingly, the Brazen Head never turned a profit but Donogh enjoyed coming home from Dublin at weekends and holding court there after greyhound racing at the Markets Field. Although 'on the dry' he would have wished from time to time to be his own best customer. The night the Brazen Head opened he was standing at the bar with my mother, admiring all the changes. He turned to her and said: "Y'know, Hilda this is the second time I have decorated this place. The first time was many years ago when I was drinking and I grabbed a fire extinguisher, hopped it off the bar counter to activate it and then proceeded to spray the bottles and wall of the bar!"'

'Donogh entered Dáil Éireann on 25 May 1954, the day I was born in Hatch Street in Dublin. You wouldn't find too many full-time politicians in those days as the salary for a TD was meagre, so Donogh continued with his engineering and got involved in building. His early days in national politics were inauspicious; he wasn't making any progress politically and he remained a TD for longer than he would have wished. Presumably, there was a fear of his continued drinking and reckless behaviour among the powers that be in Fianna Fáil.

'One should bear in mind as well the spartan conditions in Leinster House in those days. This was long before the mobile phone invasion and there was one secretary to three TDs. There were no researchers, and just the one phone for several TDs. I remember my father complaining about having to queue for up to an hour to make his nightly call home. Seemingly the Dáil restaurant and bar left a lot to be desired as well, but at least he could get a drink in the bar.'

AL FINUCANE'S CROWD
Daragh was a keen soccer supporter: 'I became a great fan of League Of Ireland soccer from the age of seven and would attend almost all the Limerick AFC soccer matches at the

home of Limerick soccer, the Markets Field. Limerick AFC were a highly respected League of Ireland team during those years. Al Finucane, Joe O'Mahony, Andy McEvoy and Kevin Fitzpatrick were my heroes. I tried to go to their away matches too, and when Donogh became Parliamentary Secretary he got a state car with two drivers, which was dead handy for taking me to quite a few away fixtures.

'I remember one of the first questions I asked my father was: 'Dad, what does the AFC in Limerick AFC stand for?"

'"Al Finucane's Crowd, that's what it stands for, Daragh," was his reply, and I believed him in my innocence. Al Finucane, Captain of Limerick, was capped several times for Ireland and in his prime turned down a lucrative offer to move to the great Glasgow Celtic team managed by Jock Stein. Al was perhaps the most successful of all home-grown soccer players in Limerick.

'I don't think my father had ever been to a soccer match in his life when he called me one evening from Dublin and said, "Listen, what would you think if I became President of the Football Association of Ireland?"

'I said, "You must be joking, that'd be great." So without ever having attended a soccer match he became President of the FAI. It was quite incredible. He didn't say it to me at the time, but I could see where he was going with this. Most of the support for Limerick AFC came from the housing estates like Garryowen, Ballananty and St Mary's Park – a working-class attendance which trudged every Sunday to the Markets Field.

'As President of the FAI, he took me along to many soccer internationals at Dalymount Park. On one occasion he did come to see Limerick play, but the cachet for Donogh was following high-profile people into the position of President of the FAI, proper men like Oscar Traynor, his immediate predecessor.

'The FAI wanted somebody high-profile as their President and although my father didn't chase the position, the FAI were delighted to have him. His appointment strengthened his association with working-class Limerick and there's no doubt he garnered quite a few votes from it. I, however, probably got the best end of the deal, attending Dalymount Park on a regular basis and getting to Wembley Stadium for the Tottenham Hotspur versus Chelsea FA Cup Final in 1967.

'When he was appointed Parliamentary Secretary to the Minister for Finance and put in charge of the Board of Works, Donogh was almost defiantly intent on spending money, a characteristic that was to endure throughout his political career. Donogh loved to spend. His first announcement was an extravagant one; he was going to drain the River Shannon, top to toe, much to the consternation of the then Minister for Finance. He wasn't gong to be intimidated by any superior or civil servant. Quite rightly, he felt that after spending ten years as a TD on the back benches, this was an overdue opportunity for him to effect change and make a difference.

'He was always acutely aware of the class system that existed in Limerick, even in sport. Donogh was a fabulous all-round athlete and loved his swimming and water polo; he was passionate about water. The class distinction was quite strong in his own family. When he lined out to play rugby for Shannon his mother frowned upon the move and urged him to find a better class of club to play with.

'Donogh loved to tell the story of the bickering Limerick

couple where the wife was complaining to her husband that he spent too much time supporting Shannon Rugby Club. "Michael," says the wife, "I really think you love Shannon more than you love me."

"Mary" says the husband, "I fuckin' loves Garryowen more than I loves you!"

Donogh O'Malley was not an intensely religious man; he would dutifully attend Sunday Mass with his family, but religious matters did not weigh heavily on him. The Sunday ritual was the eleven o'clock Mass at the Jesuits. During the sermon Donogh would step outside and smoke a cigarette and slip back before he was missed – or so he thought. The priests were aware of his movements and took some amusement from them. After Mass we would visit his mother at Auburn House on O'Connell Avenue. Donogh referred to this ritual as the 'Thirteenth Station of the Cross – Donogh visits his afflicted mother.'

Daragh says that Sunday afternoon was Donogh's only real rest time: 'After Sunday lunch he would head to bed with all the Sunday newspapers and sleep for a few hours. In the evenings, when my mother might take a glass of wine with dinner. I remember Donogh often breaking out in a cold sweat. His craving for drink was considerable at certain moments: he never fully escaped from the lure of alcohol, or stepped back over that invisible line.

'My father's three main passions in life were politics, gambling and alcohol, not necessarily in that order or even in any order. It was common for him to have £100 or £200 pound bets on a dog or horse. Life at home was very good; he loved coming down from Dublin at the weekends and we looked forward very much to seeing him. There was never an argument or aggression in our house whether he was drinking or not.

'It seems to me now that my father stopped growing up at the age of twenty-five, what would be called arrested emotional development these days. Whether this was a consequence of the alcohol abuse is hard to say; he always had a sense of devilment and mischief about him.

The only disagreement in our home would have been between me and my sister Suzanne. We had a sort of ongoing innocent argument over the merits or otherwise of Cliff Richard, her favourite. My taste and passion was for the music of Elvis Presley. I'm not sure if either one of us prevailed.'

Visits of the Elder Statesman

'Éamon de Valera and his wife Sinéad were frequent visitors to Sunville House. They would stay one or two nights in Sunville on their way to Bruree, the de Valera homestead. At first. I hadn't a clue who this tall straight-postured elderly man was. I remember he would fraternise with my sister and me, coming into my bedroom and looking at my soccer pictures on the wall and going into Suzanne's room to see the pop stars on her wall. Only later did I come to realise how genuinely interested he really was. De Valera had a quality only great men possess – the ability to make ordinary people feel important. Dev made *us* feel important and of course we liked him for it. Sinéad wrote fairy tales and stories and always wanted to know what we were reading. Every time she published a new book of her marvellous fairy stories, signed copies would always turn up at Sunville.

'Donogh loved the idea of having Dev in his house: entertaining him, tea and biscuits in the afternoon, long walks in the garden, the two deep in conversation. I think Donogh fancied himself as an elder statesman, even though he was only a TD at the time. At heart, my father was not a republican. His family background points to an Irish Parliamentary tradition in the mould of Parnell and John Redmond.

'He wanted to understand the republican mind, however, and the impetus behind that vision. De Valera was a big asset to him in this respect because he got a rare insight into the soul of republicanism and the republican ideal. He also gained understanding and insight from talks with Neil Blaney, a man who lived at the coal-face of republicanism in Donegal. Donogh would often say, "Neil Blaney *is* Fianna Fáil!"

'Charles Haughey, Brian Lenihan, Neil Blaney and Kevin Boland were also frequent visitors to Sunville. These were the so-called "men in mohair suits", an inappropriate pejorative reference. They were men of vision, led by Seán Lemass, who were attuned to the needs of a changing Ireland, mindful of the need to educate people to university level, have a comprehensive health service, improve the situation of the poor, and not lose consciousness of the working man. These five men created what has become the Celtic Tiger.

The resignation of Lemass and the ensuing maneuvering to find a replacement were a considerable blow to Fianna Fáil. Granted, his health was declining more than his colleagues realised; but sadly Jack Lynch, the compromise Taoiseach, did not have the capabilities to steer the country through what happened subsequently. He came to rely very heavily on Des O'Malley, but ultimately Charlie Haughey was by far too cunning for them all.'

5

'PRINCE OF THOMOND'
O'MALLEY THE LOCAL POLITICIAN

TRADE UNION UNREST AND UNEMPLOYMENT 1945-70
The employment situation in the city of Limerick after 1945 was precarious. Over-production was the biggest culprit, with too many factories engaged in producing the same class of goods. The bacon, flour-milling, clothing, and shoe industry reflected this trend, even though the ITGWU in Limerick continued to grow.

By mid-1942, the *Limerick Leader* wrote that the bacon industry was in an ominous position in Limerick. There was a decrease of 27% in the pig industry in the Twenty-Six Counties. It noted that 60% of the pork butchers in the city were unemployed.

The economic malaise in the country meant that prices had risen twice as fast as wages between 1939 and 1942. There was labour unrest in the city, most notably in the port of Limerick, which was being bypassed by industrialists. There was an unfair perception that labour problems in the city were scaring industrialists away. Limerick City Council proposed several projects which would develop temporary employment. The government was encouraging proposals to develop industries with export potential.

The working classes found a very useful ally in Donogh O'Malley when he took his place on the local council. He focused on condensed milk and dairying for development, because of Limerick's established advantage in these areas. He noted: 'They should try and click with something that had not been thought of yet in the export line. There were ample funds available for such a purpose.' He argued that tourism was another area that should be encouraged.

The traditional industries of Limerick – Ranks Flour, Limerick Clothing Factory, the meat factories – were in decline. Ranks suffered from a 28% drop in consumption. Mattersons Bacon and Canning factory made redundant 120 workers in 1967 and closed down the bacon section of the factory. In 1950 Shaws was sold to Clover Meats, which itself closed in 1977 with the loss of 500 jobs. When the workers at Mattersons went on strike without pay, Donogh took out a loan to pay their wages. That cost him about £12,000, a massive sum in those times.

New industries opened, such as Krups in 1964, but they masked the reality of overall unemployment. The transition from the traditional industries of the city to those of the high-technology multinationals was gradual but inexorable. The loss of the old jobs also brought an end to an entire way of life for many Limerick workers who identified proudly with their workplaces. The declining fortunes of the Limerick dock labourers was emblematic of the changing times.

THE DOCK LABOURERS

Limerick dock labourers had the reputation of being tough, belligerent and hard-drinking. The nature and unpredictability of their job contributed to this perception. Their work was dirty and physically demanding but the men took a certain pride in their toughness. They might have weeks or months of waiting for a ship to dock, followed by the pressure from their employers to unload the ship quickly and efficiently. They worked long hours with no protection from the elements, no sick time (missing a day meant the loss of a day's pay) and little social acceptance.

They frequented their own pubs along the Dock Road – Halveys, Ryans, Hanleys, Brenns. Here they might mingle with sailors, sea captains, and workers from Ranks and McMahons. The nature of the work forced them to become physically resilient and if they got rowdy things might get quickly out of hand. Older men would go to the quieter pubs to enjoy a pint before going home.

Donogh O'Malley had an easy rapport with these men. He played rugby against many of them and respected their toughness and capacity for hard work and drink. When he went on drinking binges, he was welcome in their public houses when city centre pubs (sensibly) feared to let him in.

O'Malley rarely got in trouble among these men since they could easily subdue him. There was a mutual respect. They knew about O'Malley's generosity to their wives and families and his innumerable efforts to improve their conditions. They would never want for food, thanks to him.

O'Malley was familiar with the insecurities that the dockers faced. Apart from the efforts of the Dock Labourers Society, there was little or no provision for their families. He drew attention to this at a meeting of the city council:

I believe that the dockers are a much maligned section of the community and generally other people are not aware of the periodic type of work they get. The dockers here work on and off and they stand in a unique position as far as payment of social welfare benefits are concerned. In Limerick there are 250 dockworkers and their families. Since the prosperity of the port has fallen off, they have been particularly hard hit.

The Softest Touch in Limerick

'Donogh made his mark almost immediately in local politics in the city of Limerick,' says his son Daragh. 'It didn't take long for word to circulate in the housing estates throughout Limerick that "Dunnick" was the man to go to if you wanted something done. If you needed a medical card, a corporation house, to get a son into the guards, to get a son or husband out of jail for Christmas, to get a daughter into nursing, a son off an assault charge or to the bring the corpse of a relative back from Camden Town for burial, all that was required was "a letter from Dunnick".

'Whatever your political leanings, you could always approach Donogh in the street or line up at his Saturday or Monday-morning clinics, which he called his "Confessions". "I will be hearing Confessions on Saturday morning, Mam. Come in and see me then," was an oft-heard cant. The line outside his office on a clinic day ran from O'Connell Street around the corner into Glentworth Street and he revelled in the huge numbers coming to see him.

'He got a great kick doing turns for people who he knew

did not vote for him. "I got his son into the guards. I wouldn't mind but he's black Fine Gael." This was parish-pump politics at its best, taking care of and looking out for every member of your constituency. It's not hard to imagine his frustration therefore – even though his vote increased at each election – that he was still passed over when it came to Cabinet promotion and advancement within the Party.'

Legendary *Irish Times* columnist John Healy called O'Malley 'the softest touch in Limerick' and he became a magnet for the poor and unemployed.

'His main vote came from the less well-off areas of Limerick,' Daragh adds. 'He didn't get that many votes in the Ennis Road – that's for sure – where he had moved to from Corbally.

'The aspect Donogh loved most of all about politics was the elections, with the uncertainty, excitement and the anticipation of the outcome. He was always a little bit worried that his constituents in Limerick would let him down. There was no basis for this in reality, since he was always going to get well over his required quota of first-preference votes. He never presumed that he was going to be returned automatically, and that was a huge motivating factor for him to keep working the canvass, to keep driving himself on.

'Predictably, he increased his vote at every election. He courted the poorer end of society in Limerick; he became their biggest advocate and friend and his respect for the people of Ballynanty and St Mary's Park in the Island Field was remarkable. He was on first-name terms with most of his voters and knew which way each household voted.

'He would say to me when we were driving through St Mary's Park, "See that blue house, Dar, four number ones in there. That red house there, no good to me, they say they gave me a number one but they all voted Labour." This was reflected also in his early rugby club loyalties; his beloved Shannon RFC was made up of working-class players and he also gave loving support to a similarly-styled Bohemians RFC, as well as the Blue Star Swimming Club which was based at Corbally Baths.'

'Not a Fucking Inch!'

Broadcaster Arthur Quinlan remembers O'Malley as a local man with local preoccupations although later on he was a minister with a department in Dublin. Much of Quinlan's broadcasting and reporting work for RTÉ was focused on Munster and the mid-west and he was one of a small group of journalists who would meet Donogh when he owned the Brazen Head. O'Malley liked to hold court there on his weekly return from Dublin.

'There was considerable pressure being put on by the Americans in relation to the Shannon stopover. Speculation was growing that the Yanks would go directly to Dublin and bypass Shannon altogether.

'We had a number of discussions about this. There were four of us: myself, Tom Tobin, Noel Smith and Cormac Liddy. Out of that group only Cormac and myself are still alive. The question we kept asking Donogh was: what was he going to do about the Americans.

'"What are you going to give the Yanks this time, Donogh?"

'"I can't tell you now but I'll write it down," he said. So he wrote the answer down on the back of four pieces of paper with our names on each one.

"The results of the count will be made known shortly," he went on.

'So there we were in the Brazen Head and I remember the time. It was exactly 11:45pm.

'And the date was 1 November 1965.

'Donogh made a big show about this so-called count.

'Finally he announced: "The result of the count is: *not a fucking inch!*"'

6

The First Real Taste of Power

From the 1920s on, Irish cultural and political institutions were ill-equipped and unprepared to cope with popular new cultural forms. This collision of different worlds was well captured by Francis Stuart in his autobiographical novel, *Black List, Section H*. The protagonist, H, was interned during the Civil War for his Republican activities. The outcome of the war, as he saw it, scarcely mattered, since:

> …either under de Valera or Griffith, art, religion and politics would still be run by those who, at best, used them to give power, prestige and a good living, and, at worst,…as a means towards a sterile high-toned conformism.

The hostility shown by the clergy to the anti-Treatyites was remarked upon by a young Seán Lemass in the *Irish Independent* of 14 March 1925:

> Whenever the Irish people came within sight of achieving national independence, the full political power of the church was flung against them and forced them back. That political power

must be destroyed if our national victory is ever to be won...

We are opening the campaign now against the political influence of the Church. If we succeed in destroying that influence we will have done good work for Ireland and, I believe, for the Catholic religion in Ireland.

This was a courageous comment by the future Taoiseach, but after Fianna Fáil came to power in the 1930s the clergy remained influential. The fact that Ireland remained an overtly Catholic country is often blamed on Éamon de Valera, but in reality all the political Parties were reluctant to challenge the power of the hierarchy.

We can thank Limerick broadcaster and author, Arthur Quinlan, for providing the definitive reason why the O'Malleys, staunch Cumann na nGaedheal members since the foundation of the State, switched their allegiance to Fianna Fáil in the 1930s. It was typical O'Malley pragmatism rather than ideological differences that precipitated the change. According to Quinlan:

'Desmond O'Malley Senior (Dessie's father) was an ambitious young solicitor but he became increasingly frustrated with the lack of opportunity, as he saw it, in the Fine Gael Party in Limerick. Morgan McMahon, the timber merchant, was a successful businessman and chairman of the Party, formerly Cumann na nGaedheal, that became Fine Gael in 1933.

'Des and Morgan would have been quite friendly of course. "There's not a great future for a young solicitor in this

Party," he told McMahon. "I think I'd have a better future with Fianna Fáil."

"Des, if you feel that way," said Morgan. "Go and join them with my blessing." Quinlan later confirmed with both men that this was indeed the reason why allegiance was changed. 'There was nothing more to it than that,' Quinlan says.

According to Fianna Fáil's Paddy Kiely, 'Anything Donogh achieved did not come easy. 'Twas rough enough on him when he started out in politics; no one wanted him because they were afraid of his tearaway reputation. In 1954 he won the convention by just six votes.' His older brother Desmond, who also served as Mayor of Limerick, was very useful to him politically, and the respect accorded him by both de Valera and Lemass was well established. Donogh was aware of this and while he used it to his advantage, more often than not in those years, he severely tested the patience of Desmond. When his drinking was at its worst, few would have envisaged a Cabinet position for him. He was living very close to the edge, making enemies in the Party and inadvertently alienating political allies.

His reputation for drink and the stories surrounding his drinking exploits took on a life of their own and preceded him to Dublin. Lemass was undeterred and prepared to promote O'Malley because he took a liking to him and he could always call on Desmond to keep a watchful eye on his dissolute tendencies. In truth, O'Malley was moving away from binge drinking and it showed in his work-rate as Parliamentary Secretary to the Minister for Finance, to which post he was appointed in December 1961.

It could be argued that he found his first real taste of power compelling, even more so when sobriety became the norm for him. Dealing with the Board of Works gave O'Malley experience in working – and working through – the civil service. He was indifferent to detailed administrative work and clashed with the stifling bureaucracy. His flamboyance and his relative youth and restlessness prevailed in most cases. His reputation as an aggressive quick-minded decision-maker made him the darling of the electorate. It would take considerably longer to convince the civil servants.

MINISTER FOR HEALTH 1965–6
In a *Guardian* interview on 13 May 1960, Seán Lemass said:

> We pride ourselves on being a progressive, enter-
> prising people, concerned mainly with the future,
> busily engaged in building up our economy,
> developing agricultural and industrial production
> and exports, and providing jobs to keep our young
> men and women at home. We are not content with
> our progress up to date; we are doing our very best
> to promote a vigorous expanding economy and
> we are working for this development in a spirit of
> confidence and self-reliance.

'Ireland is catching up with the twentieth century,' wrote Norman St John-Stevas in the *Catholic Herald* in June 1960. Seán Lemass finally became Taoiseach in 1959, at the age of sixty, thirty years after he was first elected to the Dáil. Like O'Malley in Education, his time as leader of the country was relatively short, 1959–66. In that time he strove to direct government policy away from the provincialism of de Valera's dreary vision.

While mindful of maintaining continuity in Cabinet, he was responsive to the period of unprecedented change during which he led the country. The make-up of his last Cabinet reflects this willingness to promote a new, younger breed of minister. He appointed four new men to this Cabinet – O'Malley to Education, George Colley, first to Education and later to Industry and Commerce, Joe Brennan to Posts and Telegraphs and Seán Flanagan to Health. He also appointed five new parliamentary secretaries.

Health was O'Malley's first ministerial position, and he took over from Seán MacEntee, who was asked to stand down by Lemass before the 1965 election. The older politician had perhaps stayed on too long and Lemass was anxious to retire older ministers. Health service issues were predominant in the 1965 general election, and Fine Gael, in their policy document *Winning Through To A Just Society* (rebranded as *Towards a Just Society* for the 1969 election), issued a stinging criticism of the quality and organisation of existing health services. If elected, Fine Gael promised to extend medical services to all but the wealthiest 15 per cent of the population.

On his arrival in the department, O'Malley agreed to publish a White Paper outlining the changes considered necessary in the health services. The White Paper, *The Health Services and Their Further Development*, was published in January 1966. A considerable portion of the White Paper focused on detailing improvements in services and proposing administrative changes in the hospital service and ways of paying for the increasing cost of health services. The government's decision to introduce a choice of doctor in the medical service was reaffirmed.

Introducing the debate on the White Paper in the Dáil, O'Malley argued that the county was too small a unit for the organisation of many health services and advocated the development of regional boards as 'the logical outcome, not only of the other proposals in the White Paper, but of the long-term trend in the administration of the health services'. He promised legislation to implement the White Paper by autumn 1966. However, he became Minister for Education in August 1966, and not surprisingly, the process of negotiation and preparation for the appearance of the bill stalled.

Though his stay in Health was short, O'Malley was quick to react to Dr Bryan Alton, a senator and leading medical spokesman, who claimed that the great majority of the medical profession in the country were anxious for fee-per-service.

In the Senate, O'Malley criticised Alton for alerting doctors on the issue of payment, and he berated 'hot-heads,' and 'wild-catters' in the IMA (Irish Medical Association) for stirring up trouble. In a subsequent television interview O'Malley claimed that 5 per cent of dispensary doctors treated some of their patients like 'pigs'. He warned the profession that he did not want 'to use the big stick', and that he would not be 'blackmailed into coming down on any particular side'. He said, 'There seems to be a lobby working among the medical profession about a certain method of payment. This will not influence me in the slightest.'

In the senate he continued in similar vein:

> If the doctors are trying to influence me unduly, and trying to work up a hysterical lobby, they are dealing with the wrong man on this occasion. I can

tell you that much. They will not frighten me with some of the threats that I have heard and some of the methods which are being adopted.

The lines were clearly drawn at this point and a showdown between the minister and the medical profession was imminent. This was averted when O'Malley moved to Education, to the relief of the medical profession, which found the confrontational Limerickman more than they could handle. O'Malley's appointment to Education was one of the last landmark decisions of the Lemass administration.

'MURROE IS IN THE PAST'
Tom O'Donnell, former Fine Gael TD for Limerick East, Minister for the Gaeltacht and MEP, served in the Dáil with Donogh O'Malley from October 1961, when he was first elected, until O'Malley's death in March 1968.

Despite being on opposite sides of the House in Dáil Éireann, O'Donnell and O'Malley had a very friendly personal relationship, based on mutual respect and a shared commitment to the socio-economic development of Limerick and the Shannon region. In an interview, Tom affectionately recalled his first stormy encounter with Donogh in Murroe and his final poignant meeting with him during the Clare by-election:

'My first encounter with Donogh on the 1961 election campaign was remarkable. On the last Sunday evening of the campaign, there was a Mission on in Murroe. The whole parish was there, needless to say, and representatives of the political Parties were gathered to address people when they came out after Mass.

'Being young at the time, I had a youthful, exuberant crowd with me, and I spoke first. There was a bit of heckling going on and the tension was fairly high. Donogh then arrived and he got up to speak. He started in his usual inimitable fashion, lashing out at the Opposition and their lack of policy and so on.

'One of my supporters got a bit excited about what Donogh was saying. At that time there were massive numbers leaving Ireland, in the region of 50,000 a year. Next thing anyway my man shouts up at Donogh.

'"Mr O'Malley, what about the thousand people a week leaving our shores?"'

'Donogh carried on and ignored the heckling. But my man kept at it. "Mr O'Malley, what about the cream of our young boys and girls leaving in their thousands every week?"

'After about the third time Donogh paused, eyeballed the heckler, and said: "'Twas a great pity that 1001 didn't leave last week!"

'The timing and delivery was pure theatre. It was a brilliant put-down, devoid of malice. But that was Donogh, quick-minded and sharp as a tack.

'On my first day in the Dáil, he was made a Parliamentary Secretary (now called a junior minister) to the Minister for Finance, with responsibility for the Board of Works. We met on the corridor and he invited me down to his office. We were chatting away about various matters when he said to me:

'"Now Tom, Murroe is in the past, the campaign is over. We're in different Parties, but we have one thing in common. We both represent the constituency of Limerick East. We've got to work together now in the interests of our constituency."

'He was a great character that way, and Party lines were dispensed with.'

'It was in 1966 that a Cabinet reshuffle saw him take over as Minster for Education, where he made his real mark. His free post-primary education and free buses were a tremendous breakthrough and completely revolutionised Irish education in subsequent years.'

'The Country Cut no Dash'

Bruce Arnold was born in England and came to Ireland in the late 1950s to study at TCD. He never returned home but remained an unrepentant Englishman. He has his critics, this Englishman who has lived here for more than fifty years but refuses to become an Irishman. It's a criticism that never troubled him even though he has grappled with his place as an Englishman living in Ireland.

As a political commentator he is passionate, even emotional, as seen in his withering assessment of Charlie Haughey. On the other hand, he was quite soft on Jack Lynch. He has written several books on literature and art.

His love for Ireland informs the best of his work and he is uniquely placed as a dispassionate witness to Irish politics for the last four decades of the twentieth century:

'Writing about Ireland for English readers was fraught with difficulty. The country cut no dash. Ireland believed that it had no natural resources. People were still being exported at a steady rate, which, although it had come down form the high point of the late 1950s, was still a bit depressing. Many were living on remittance money. There was a tendency to glory in the achievements of Irish people outside Ireland, but there was no parallel sense, within the country, of dignity, excitement, progress.

'We had been through the dark period post-war, the period of unemployment, emigration, continuing poverty. And it had culminated in the mid-1950s, in a kind of despair as to whether independence had worked at all. As a young observer, I shared in the doubt and wondered if Ireland was a viable entity? Many others doubted it, not least those who governed us. And it gave enormous power to the Roman Catholic Church. On many issues its leading figure, John Charles McQuaid, appeared almost to have a seat at the government table, and a hand in the making of government policy.

'The *Guardian* was well regarded by Irish politicians. The wave of new men – Charles Haughey, Donogh O'Malley, Brian Lenihan – felt that their noble works should be noted in an English newspaper which was not too right-wing, like the *Daily Telegraph*, and not too establishment, like *The Times*. And so they asked me to press conferences and told me what they were doing. And I wrote about it.

'Perhaps the most significant thing about the 1960s was not an achievement at all; rather it was the simple result of the grimness of the 1950s: an absence of desire to look back. The Irish, who have shown in recent years, and throughout the past thirty years as well, an intense and sustained interest in their own past, behaved for the first time differently during the 1960s, and concentrated on a future which was concerned with the prospect of economic growth and development, the new world of television, liberation from censorship, and a political and social life which was increasingly disposed to believe in promises.

'It was still a deeply Catholic society. *Ne Temere* prevailed.

The Catholic Church retained enormous power. The ideology and practice of the left, embraced by the Labour Party, represented still by other left-wing factions, remained a supposed threat, and was significant in the general election result of 1969, when Fine Gael and Labour failed to achieve the necessary transfer of votes because of mutual distrust about the extent of left-wing ideology in the Labour Party.'

Arnold was a consistent and penetrating observer of political life in Ireland during the early to mid-1960s. His job would have brought him into frequent meetings with Cabinet ministers and front-bench TDs. Even though there was an enduring suspicion of journalists among leading politicians it was essential to tolerate them, if not cultivate friendship with them.

Arnold was on reasonably good terms with Donogh O'Malley. 'He was friendly and sympathetic to me, unlike many others. I did an interview in his office and I think he was suspicious (as were most of the Irish politicians) of British people. Many politicians believed that the British were carrying out surveillance in Ireland, which was not the case in the early 1960s. I would have known Donogh from about 1962–3 through to his death. Since I wrote for the *Guardian* at the time, members of the Cabinet were very anxious to have what they were doing covered in that paper. A lot of Irish people read it.

'Donogh was quite close to Haughey, but wouldn't have supported the republican stance that Haughey became enmeshed in. He would have been against that. My outstanding impression of him was that he was ill, he wasn't a fit man and it showed. I don't know what he died of; clearly he had been off the drink for quite some time.'

7

Readiness for Change
Donogh O'Malley in Education

In an article in the *Irish Press* on 2 May 1957, then Minister for Education Jack Lynch wrote:

> I cannot help feeling that if we were to take a greater interest in our system of education the teachers would feel less isolated in their battle for the minds of the country's youth, would feel more at one with the community generally and that far-reaching effects might be achieved which are evidently not being achieved at present.

According to journalist John Healy, writing in *Magill*:

> Education is the ministry which really shapes the nation and if you have ambitions to be a nation shaper you reach for the department of education and go to work. Not every politician of my time would agree. Most see Finance as the creative ministry, and Charles Haughey in his day demonstrated what a man with an imaginative turn of mind could do.

He went on to say that O'Malley 'lusted after the portfolio'. This is an exaggeration and it diminishes O'Malley's genuine long-time interest in education. Up to the 1950s, education was not seen as a high-profile ministry. The department was narrow in its perspective, Irish-speaking, located in the centre of Dublin. The role of the minister was largely a passive one, with the department left to its own devices. The foundation for O'Malley's achievement in education was laid by Patrick Hillery, and, to a lesser extent, by George Colley.

Readiness for change had been created by Dr Patrick Hillery (b. 1923), a medical doctor, who was Minister for Education from 1959 to 1965. His contribution has been overlooked largely because of O'Malley's charismatic and confrontational implementation of the free education scheme.

The system of secondary education in the 1960s was an outdated relic, out of line with the economic and social development of the time. The system was divisive: intelligent children continued from primary school into a secondary school if their parents could afford the fees, or if a particular religious order waived them and the children passed the entrance exam. The alternative, for the less academic and those who could not pay, was the vocational school or 'tech', as it was pejoratively called. The stigma associated with the tech was disheartening and the effectiveness of its role as education-provider was undermined by that stigma.

As Minister for Education, Hillery believed that entry to post-primary education should be free, but his desire for reform was thwarted by the Department of Finance's fear of cost, and the Catholic Church's dread of losing control over education. Lemass was sympathetic to his views and supported the setting up a pilot scheme that, it was intended, would later be extended to the rest of the country.

Hillery may not have been as effective as he would have wished, but his efforts represented the successful beginning of state involvement in post-primary education. He also transformed the passive uninvolved image of the minister in Irish education. In his quiet unassuming way, Dr Hillery made a definitive statement of intent: the traditional relationship between church and state shifted significantly with the introduction of comprehensive schooling. Subsequent ministers would benefit from this shift, especially O'Malley.

I HAVE LIVED IN IMPORTANT PLACES

> I have lived in important places, times
> When great events were decided
> Patrick Kavanagh, 'Epic' (1938)

Paddy Hillery laughs easily. 'I don't feel like working any more,' he says, commenting on the stream of requests by radio shows for his participation, queries about a history of Clare and invitations to take part in discussions about education. 'Where were they fifteen years ago?' he asks. 'Did someone tell them I'm ready to depart the scene? I think I'm finished,' he says, laughing heartily.

Hillery would now much prefer to be playing golf with his four-ball pals. The legs are not quite up to all the walking, or so he says. 'Now we meet for lunch every Tuesday instead. I think we'd all rather be playing. I have made great friendships playing the game.'

Perhaps it's no coincidence that one of his favourite poems

is Patrick Kavanagh's 'Epic'. His own career in politics has been an epic if unheralded one. 'When I'm travelling I like to read those lines although I have them committed to memory. W.B. Yeats is also a favourite of mine, but Kavanagh strikes the right note.'

Hillery is inextricably tied to his native County Clare; the family home where he was born is still there. He would like to visit it more often than time allows. It was in his early days in Clare that he became acquainted with Donogh O'Malley.

'I remember when Donogh used to compete in the swimming and diving exhibitions down in Doolin. He was an accomplished swimmer, and he was mad for the water. There was one memorable night when he stood up and sang a song, "Santa Lucia", at one of the hotels in Lisdoonvarna. I suppose he wasn't what you'd call a gifted singer but once he got going there was no stopping him!'

'I have very fond memories of Donogh, but I was closer to Dessie, his older brother. He used to come down a lot to Spanish Point. Of course Donogh was a most entertaining man. He did very well in the politics but he was fond of a bit of sport and craic.'

Paddy Hillery gave up medicine in 1951 to become de Valera's running mate in County Clare. When Lemass replaced Dev as Taoiseach, Hillery pursued a brilliant ministerial career in 1959 in Seán Lemass's 'Brave New Ireland'.

Hillery, who was appointed Minister for Education in 1959, set out a vision of educational opportunity in 1963 when he established the comprehensive schools, offering both academic and applied subjects to all the pupils within a ten-mile radius. He set up the Commission on Higher Education whose report, *Investment In Education* (1965), was a landmark in shaping Irish education for the rest of the twentieth century. His comprehensive schools initiated and set the course for O'Malley's achievement in education.

Hillery was Ireland's first Minister for Labour in 1965, and presided over the formation of the training agency Anco, the forerunner of FÁS. He could have succeeded Seán Lemass as Taoiseach; he was asked to put his name forward by Lemass and others, but he refused. It is likely he would have replaced Lemass with unanimous Party approval as he had all the qualities: the age, the experience and the integrity. He negotiated Ireland's accession to the EEC in 1972, when he was Minister for External Affairs. For most people the enduring image of Hillery is the signing of our Treaty of Accession to the EEC.

Hillery became President of Ireland in 1976 and served two terms until 1990. He had the presence of a statesman accompanied by a distinctive panache and sense of humour.

Hillery's record in government ranks him as one of the architects of modern Ireland. His contribution to education alone would have ensured his place in history. The key principles he set out in the 1960s have stood the test of time.

For all of his achievements and belated accolades, Hillery never lost his compassion and his pronounced human touch. This was never more clearly in evidence than when Donogh O'Malley died:

'I was in charge of the election in the Clare section. Kevin Boland was to be speaking that morning in Sixmilebridge, but Donogh came instead. I will never forget what happened to Donogh that day. I was very upset. It never bothered me that Donogh got all the acclaim in relation to the free education.

Sure we all knew what went into the creation of it. What did the acclaim matter to him, or indeed to anyone, after he was taken from us so suddenly and so swiftly?'

> Till Homer's ghost came whispering to my
> mind.
> He said: I made the Iliad from such
> A local row. Gods make their own importance.
>
> Patrick Kavanagh, 'Epic' (1938)

Two observations dominated the 1965 report, *Investment In Education*, a study based on the work of Professor Paddy Lynch and W.J. Hyland, a distinguished statistician: there was an over-abundance of small rural primary schools, and there was an inadequate provision of post-primary education, which was run essentially by private, religious interests.

When George Colley took over the Education brief he was under the distinct but incorrect impression that Lemass was about to take measure to amalgamate a number of smaller primary schools. Opposition from the teachers and the Catholic hierarchy left no room for manoeuvre, despite Colley's best efforts. The initiative meandered and stumbled along, with no significant decision-making. That was to change when O'Malley succeeded Colley in Education in July 1966.

Conflict with Limerick VEC

O'Malley was barely two weeks in office when he attended a specially convened meeting of the Limerick City Vocational Education Committee (VEC). There was always an element of ambiguity about the governance of vocational schools, which were unique in that they were publicly owned and managed by representatives appointed by the local authorities. They were in principle non-denominational, but in practice the Churches managed to have a significant role in appointments to committees.

Under the terms of the Vocational Education Act 1930, the VEC had autonomous legislation which enabled it to operate as a corporate body independent of its parent body, with power to acquire and hold land for the purposes of its powers and duties. The Catholic Church sought assurances that its influence would not be undermined. They were uneasy with the assumption that religious authorities might not necessarily have a say in the managing of a school system.

In Limerick, the custom of electing clergy unopposed and of returning the sitting clerical members had been established during the first twenty years of vocational education.

The new minister was greeted and congratulated by VEC members but he was in no mood for niceties. They were shocked into silence when he told them he was 'seriously perturbed by their past behaviour'. He continued:

> For a number of years I have been concerned by the committee's financial practices and by its appointment procedures with considerations other than relevant qualifications often used in the making of announcements.

He asked Seán Mac Gearailt, one of his most senior officers, to conduct a full enquiry. Mac Gearailt initially examined alleged financial irregularities, and after two months he turned his attention to the manner of making appointments;

the grading of posts; their assignment between schools; the designation of duties and the supervision of teachers' duties. The enquiry concluded in February 1967, and less than a month later, the committee was issued with a ministerial order suspending it and appointing a principal officer of the Department of Education, Pádraig Ó Ceallaigh, to perform its duties.

O'Malley might have been accused of point-scoring on these matters but the findings of the enquiry exposed the inadequacies and abuses of the process of appointments. This paved the way for ministerial reforms in 1967. It also placed O'Malley front and centre in the eyes of the Church as a man to be feared and as a direct threat to its long-standing control of local education.

8

'A Startling Innovation'
the Introduction of Free Education

On 10 September 1966, O'Malley announced that free post-primary education would be available to all families. (The text of his free education speech appears in full as an appendix on page 183) The impact was immediate, far-reaching and sensational, as O'Malley intended it to be. The reaction wasn't all favourable. T.K. Whitaker, Secretary of the Department of Finance, was incensed.

> It is astonishing that a major change in educational policy should be announced by the Minister for Education at a weekend seminar of the National Union of Journalists. This 'free schooling' policy has not been the subject of any submission to the Department of Finance, has not been approved by the government, has certainly not been examined from the financial...aspect, and therefore should have received no advance publicity, particularly of the specific and definite type involved in Mr O'Malley's statement.

Lemass was certainly aware of O'Malley's intentions, even if there was ambiguity about the wording and the implications surrounding the announcement. O'Malley wrote to Lemass:

> It was my understanding that I had your agreement to my outlining these lines of action, particularly in view of the fact that Fine Gael were planning to announce a comprehensive educational policy this week…If I was under a misapprehension in believing that I had your support for my announcement, I must apologise. I would hope, however, that what I have said will persuade you that I was right in making it and that you will give me your full support in getting my plans approved by the government.

This cleverly crafted letter took the pressure off Lemass and enabled him to maintain his tacit support for O'Malley's endeavours.

Jack Lynch, Minister for Finance, presented a different problem entirely. He had been out of the country while O'Malley was running wild with his proposals. O'Malley's contempt for his office was one thing; his continued defence of the seemingly indefensible maddened Lynch still further:

> If the proposals of the Minister for Education are to be approved, there will be no alternative to the imposition of new taxation; this may have serious economic reactions. To describe the scheme as 'free' is misleading. The scheme really means that many parents at present paying moderate school

fees voluntarily will have to pay an equal or greater amount compulsorily in the form of additional taxation.

O'Malley remained unperturbed by this caustic assessment. In any case, there was no retreating from the commitment once it was made. The wave of popular enthusiasm in support of the scheme ensured that. O'Malley's trump card was the flood of mail that arrived each morning in the Department of Education, and he took great delight in flaunting this unequivocal nationwide support. In the Senate he made this defiant declaration:

> No one is going to stop me introducing my scheme next September. I know I am up against opposition and serious organised opposition but they are not going to defeat me on this. I shall tell you further that I shall expose them and I shall expose their tactics on every available occasion whoever they are. I see my responsibilities to the Irish people and the Irish children. No vested interest or group, whoever they may be, at whatever level, will sabotage what every reasonable-minded man considers to be a just scheme.

The speed of the announcement gave little opportunity to the managerial bodies to examine the implications of free education. The alternative proposal from Fine Gael was effectively ignored. Heated exchanges in the Dáil between O'Malley and Fine Gael's Patrick Lindsay and James Dillon confirmed that the Opposition had been caught napping.

Dillon was frustrated; the Limerick man had outsmarted the danger men in Opposition, specifically Garret FitzGerald.

THE DÁIL DEBATES FREE EDUCATION
When the Committee on Finance resumed consideration of the estimates for public service spending for the year ending 31 March 1967, O'Malley opened with a spirited defence of his free education scheme

> When in September last I announced that I would introduce a scheme of free education, the members of the principal Opposition Party told all and sundry that I was making a promise that would never be fulfilled. They asked where was the money going to come from. Suddenly it dawned on them that here was something that was going to be implemented and implemented in a responsible way. They then rushed out their policy for education and the scene changed overnight. The country which was bankrupt in their eyes a few weeks ago is now so opulent that the buoyancy in revenue can be expected to be such as to pay for an education plan running into many millions without any resort to additional taxation.

Patrick Lindsay, Fine Gael education spokesman, replied:

> You do not alter education or you do not improve education in bits and pieces, as this document would tend to suggest...nowhere in the course of this whole document is there

a single reference to the fundamentals of what education is. Nowhere have we got a guideline as to what the aims are in the department for primary education, for secondary education, for vocational education, or indeed as to what university education should be. This is the minister, who when he gets a public opportunity, taunts people about not having a policy, thereby suggesting he has one or will have one…What are the people going to think…of this minister who showed bravery…in Dún Laoghaire, that is not matched in this document less than two months later. Will they not describe him in the words of Disraeli in *Menjnoun* as a 'figure flitting across the stage, as a transient and embarrassed phantom'?

Mr O'Malley: I love the Disraeli bit.

Mr Lindsay: 'It is a good bit. I hope the minister is now going to break forth from the chains that were binding him while he was reading this and become the charming extrovert he usually is, so charming as to be dangerous.

Tom O'Donnell, O'Malley's friend and political rival in Limerick East, made the best of the changed circumstances. O'Donnell had a strong interest in education from his seminary years and his teaching in Dublin. His assessment of Donogh O'Malley's contribution to the policy of free education is discerning and balanced.

'It was a bold and brilliant move. Donogh was very pragmatic; he always saw the bigger picture. The idea of free education didn't originate with him but that's beside the point. He saw an opportunity to enact a massive change and he delivered on it. He knew exactly what he was doing.

'He covered all the angles; he met with the hierarchy and the clergy and eventually won their approval. Moreover, he believed in what he was doing. Where others saw obstacles he saw opportunity. Of course it didn't sit well with the civil servants and members of the Cabinet, but he outmanoeuvred the lot of them.

'His announcement to the journalists heading into the weekend was a brilliant strategy. His biggest worry was that Garret (FitzGerald) might get wind of what he was doing and steal a march on him. In truth, there was no one going to deny him. Some would say it was opportunistic. I never heard Paddy Hillery say anything to that effect, and his groundwork was considerable. I would suggest that it was visionary.'

O'Donnell's questioning of the minister had more to do with the practicalities of implementing the scheme, especially in problematic towns and villages in Limerick East:

'When I'd meet Donogh outside the Dáil all I could do was smile. Ah sure, you had to. "That'll give the ******* something to think about, O'Donnell," he'd say to me, all smiles and laughter. His plan was executed to perfection.'

The mischievous youngster from the Mill Road had struck again. O'Malley's master-stroke had been effected and he could indulge his boyish sense of devilment. The same enjoyment was not experienced by Jack Lynch, whose dislike of the Limerick man was accentuated. O'Malley had won this match of wits and Lynch knew it.

Significantly, O'Malley did not consult the Church in advance. After initial dissent from the religious orders, pragmatism overcame their earlier fears. O'Malley travelled to Maynooth along with Tomás Ó Raiftearaigh, Secretary of the Department of Education, and two assistant secretaries, to discuss his policies with Cardinal Conway and Archbishop John Charles McQuaid.

By the summer of 1967, the O'Malley scheme had gained the support of the hierarchy and it was implemented that September. It was evident to the Church authorities that they stood to gain financially by embracing the scheme. Of course this acceptance did not mitigate McQuaid's dislike of O'Malley. What irritated McQuaid was the questioning of the role of the religious in education by O'Malley and other politicians:

> How little they know of the history of education or of the organisation of a school who, in myopic ignorance, have accused the Brothers and Sisters or reluctance to assist the poor. Were it not for the intelligent preparation and constant self-sacrifice of the congregations…the present system of free education could not have been even partially initiated.

Jack Lynch had replaced Seán Lemass as Taoiseach in November 1966, and O'Malley found himself isolated in his dealings with the Church. Lynch was feebly deferential to McQuaid: visits were exchanged, with McQuaid calling on Lynch at Government Buildings and Lynch returning the call to Drumcondra.

Free education may have broken the psychological and ideological taboo but it received scathing criticism from

T.K. Whitaker in particular. The criticism had merit; the scheme was pushed through quickly and with little thought of implementation and this added unnecessarily to its cost. Vocational education fell out of favour, with few pupils opting to continue in vocational schools to the Leaving Certificate. However, given the staunch conservatism and vested interests that O'Malley had to sidestep, these flaws could hardly have been avoided.

The opening up of free post-primary education to all the children of the state, and the introduction of a free school bus service in rural areas, were considerable achievements, passed and implemented in a relatively short period of time. The importance of the collaboration of the majority of the managers of existing privately-owned schools cannot be overestimated. Within seven years there was a twenty-five per cent increase in voluntary school enrolments, which ensured the continuation of voluntary secondary schools.

The scheme was successful, not simply because it was free, but because a considerable section of the population, never previously involved with post-primary education, was now aware that education was their children's right. This awareness, combined with free school transport, determined that education was no longer the preserve of the better-off.

Other changes followed. The Primary Certificate examination – the traditional entrance examination for gaining places in secondary schools – was discontinued from 1968. In December 1967, Donogh O'Malley appointed Professor Louden Ryan, an economist at TCD, to chair a tribunal on teachers' salaries. The following year the development branch of the Department of Education began publishing a journal, *Oideas*, which has stood the test of time. Its stated aim is 'to disseminate information about educational matters amongst all engaged in the work of education in Ireland' and it reaches every institution in the country that is involved in education.

Efforts by the Department of Education in early 1967 to initiate a revision of the Leaving Certificate programme, a logical corollary to the free education for all scheme, were not successful. Predictably, managerial bodies balked at the influx of students who, prior to September 1967, would have been considered academically unsuitable for secondary schools and perhaps more suited to technical education in the vocational schools.

These teething problems were inevitable and it would require time, patience and a willingness to compromise for all interests to embrace the new scheme. Similarly, the amalgamation (common enrolment) of schools in areas where two or three small secondary or vocational schools existed, had limited success and was resisted by the ASTI (Association of Secondary Teachers Ireland). The distinction between secondary and vocational schools would not easily be blurred.

'The Poor Hoor was Killed'

Donogh O'Malley and Oliver J. Flanagan engaged in a heated debate over the suitability of an anthology of short stories prescribed by the Department of Education for Intermediate Certificate English. Flanagan found two stories objectionable – 'Guests Of The Nation', by Frank O'Connor, and 'The Trout', by Sean O'Faolain – because of inappropriate language:

> This type of language might be expected in a low
> class pitch-and-toss school, but should not be

contained in a book for young children, many of whom are in their first years of preparation for, perhaps, a religious life, or to take their place in whatever profession they are going to follow... Maybe we are reaching the stage of modern teaching when everything is being modernised, but if this is the type of language to be used in our textbooks, I am sorry we did not remain old-fashioned.

On page 198, one sees the expression 'Ah for Christ's sake.' There are numerous parents who would not allow their children to use that expression. It would be wrong and improper.

The minister's response was somewhat mischievous but it was highly effective, delivered with flair and humour. In reference to 'The Trout,' O'Malley suggested that the deputy had not read the story in its entirety.

Flanagan: 'The Trout'?
O'Malley: Yes
Flanagan: From cover to cover. Very suggestive. I did not like it
O'Malley: Does the Deputy, if he has read the story, realise that it is his own vivid and excitable imagination –
Flanagan: No. Parents have written to me
O'Malley: I would point out to the Deputy that if he had read the story he would see this young girl is going into the tunnel to catch a trout and not to catch anything else. If these ideas which

the Deputy is putting into Irish minds, which no doubt, will be widely published in tomorrow's papers, are all he can find in Sean O'Faolain's 'The Trout,' which has been described also as the finest story of O'Faolain, then I can only say 'God help us,' and it is a very lucky thing that O'Faolain and O'Connor cannot combine to write a story on the proceedings here tonight and on the last day.

It is safe to say that five or ten years hence world television, to which nothing will be sacred, will be thrown open to us from many stations in the sky. It may have seemed to the committee that the responsible milieu of the classroom is, next to the home, the best place to prepare the pupils for what we must expect in a world of such open communication which is coming, if indeed it is not already upon us...It should be said that the words concerned, apart from their legal sense, do not carry, at least in Ireland, a connotation other than mild, vulgar, opprobrium. Curiously enough, if preceded by the adjective 'poor' they would express sympathy. I think the Deputy will agree with that. In the south of Ireland if one said, 'John fell down a cliff, and the poor hoor was killed –'

Flanagan: If he is a poor bastard or a poor hoor, he is still a bastard or hoor.

O'Malley: If Deputy Flanagan went down to the south of Ireland at a by-election, pulled up at the side of the road and was told: 'John fell down a cliff and the poor hoor was killed –'

Flanagan: I would say: 'Lord have mercy on him.'

O'Malley: The Deputy would say rightly: 'The Lord have mercy on him.' He would not start slagging him for using that type of language. He would say: 'The poor hoor, Lord have mercy on him.'

Flanagan: I would not; I would leave out 'poor hoor'. I do not care for that type of language.

O'Malley: I think the ordinary reasonably-minded person appreciates the fact that we are doing a good service in the teaching of English literature to our children…Anyone who has read this story would not have the slightest qualms of conscience about letting a child read it, it fits so aptly into the whole trend of the story. If the mentality of Deputy Flanagan is like that of the unfortunate girl who went into the tunnel to catch a trout, and not to catch anything else, the Lord have mercy on us all.

BUNTÚS CAINTE

One of the surprising successes was the national response to the *Buntús Cainte* Irish-language course, which O'Malley referred to in his speech announcing free education: 'I am arranging that the *Buntús* method of teaching the language shall be made available in the fullest way possible for the general public.' Asked in the Dáil if the lessons and publication were a success to that point the minister replied:

I am well satisfied with the national response to the *Buntús Cainte* lessons. All the reports which I have received, and there are very many indeed, indicate that this series of lessons and the television programme related to them have been received with the greatest enthusiasm. The fact that the lessons are scientifically based and provide adults in a pleasant way with the minimum amount of spoken Irish necessary for everyday conversation are two major reasons for their success. The third is the high degree of goodwill for the language which exists among our people.

In order to meet the demand for the booklet it has been necessary to produce five editions of it. To date 218,000 copies have been sold and the sales are continuing.

A recent assessment of *Buntús Cainte* by the noted Irish scholar and folklorist, Dáithí Ó hÓgáin, explains why the series caught the public imagination:

This series taught Irish in a new and attractive way. It placed heritage in a creative and very modern setting. It was also inclusive in that it taught Irish simply and directly, while giving a sense of the richness and variety of the Irish language.

Among the presenters were speakers of all three regional Irish dialects, who kept their own accents, yet communicated clearly and distinctly. Perhaps the most impressive thing about the series is that almost all the individuals on screen were young and were colourful in their presentation, in their style and dress.

It was based on very good linguistic research and the frequency of occurrence of words and their content were taken into account, so that those who followed the series from start to finish ended up competent Irish speakers, who could make their own of the language and express themselves succinctly through it in whatever situation.

9

University Amalgamation and Other Issues

> Everybody, I think, will agree that the university
> situation in Dublin is far from being satisfactory.
> We have here in the capital city of a small
> country what are to all intents and purposes
> two separate and very differently constituted
> university institutions, each endowed in major
> part by the State, but each ploughing its own
> furrow with virtually no provision, formal or
> even informal, for coordination of their efforts
> or the sharing by them of what must always
> be scarce but very valuable national resources.

In March 1967, another outcry followed O'Malley's surprise initiative to amalgamate Trinity College and University College Dublin. The minister was rubbing salt in old wounds since this idea had been shot down a decade earlier by John Cardinal D'Alton.

On a practical level, the free education scheme would necessarily produce a greater demand for university places, and O'Malley viewed the merger as one of the options in a search for the most rational way of accommodating the influx of putative university students.

There was no equivocation in O'Malley's announcement. He described the dual university set-up as 'a most insidious form of partition on our own doorstep,' because it segregated Catholics and Protestants. This was inflammatory language, and again O'Malley had pointedly not consulted Archbishop McQuaid. Negotiators from the two colleges began discussions on this idealistic ambition. There was strident opposition to the very idea in both institutions, but the general body of academic opinion was inclined to give the outline scheme a chance.

A major controversy was avoided, however, when Cardinal Conway and the Catholic hierarchy welcomed the proposal. Apart from remarks by Fine Gael's Pat Lindsay and a rebuke for the minister in the *Irish Independent*, little further was heard about O'Malley's proposal, and the merger negotiations stalled. Within a year O'Malley was dead and his proposal never materialised. Whether O'Malley could have pulled off another 'stroke' and brought the antagonists toward agreement will never be known. His death came at a crucial time and the opportunity to realise the last great liberal initiative of the 1960s was lost.

'Tell Us about the Frogs, Pat'
Like O'Malley, Pat Lindsay was a graduate of University College Galway. He reflected on his dealings with O'Malley in his book, *Memories*, published a year before Lindsay died in 1993:

'My opposite number in Education was Donagh (sic) O'Malley. We got on well but I opposed his closure of the small one-teacher and two-teacher village schools. It was at this time that I made a speech pointing out that the children who walked to the local school could observe the onset of spring, the appearance of flowers, the calves and lambs in the fields, and indeed the phenomenon of frogs jumping on the road after heavy rain. Fianna Fáil, never one to look a gift frog in the mouth, seized on the speech and used it afterwards to jeer me.

'On television on one famous occasion, I was taunted by Donogh O'Malley to "Tell us about the frogs, Pat." However, I enjoyed it all and believed I was right. We also clashed on the question of Dr John Charles McQuaid. Donogh attacked him about his attitude to Trinity College. I felt the attack had been somewhat snide, and I have never forgotten the kindness Dr McQuaid showed me when I was a young and unemployed teacher. I responded that I believed that McQuaid was a man of principle and that the worst people could say about him was that he adheres to fundamentals. I reckoned that this could not be a bad thing. I thought my remark had gone unnoticed but two days later I had a very charming letter from Dr McQuaid which thanked me for 'Your generous and courageous tribute in the Dáil.' He told me he was particularly grateful. 'In view of the recent barrage of criticism. I only hope I have the grace to stress the fundamentals until the end.'

'We met on a number of occasions after that and I have to say he lived up to my expectations. I was interested to hear on a radio programme in later years that the former provost of Trinity College, Dr McConnell, agreed that Dr McQuaid had been a man of principle who stuck to his fundamental beliefs.

'I have to say however, that I also liked Donogh O'Malley

enormously. I liked his panache. I liked his recklessness and above all I admired his total disregard for bureaucracy and for the Cabinet to which he belonged. His death, a terrible loss to Irish public life, saddened me enormously.'

'He Was Like a Ball of Fire'
Tony O'Dalaigh, who was private secretary to Donogh O'Malley in the Department of Education, worked with four different ministers in a five-year span. 'I knew nothing about politics,' he says. 'I had no interest in it and never read the papers. However, it was a fascinating job. Donogh was by far the most interesting of my bosses. He was well off the drink at this stage, and he was like a ball of fire. Ironically, he loved the company of drinkers, he loved to see fellas drinking. He regarded me with a bit of suspicion because I was a non-drinker. I wasn't a Pioneer, but I didn't drink. He would drink endless cups of tea and in social settings he drank large glasses of ginger ale (no ice).

'I knew O'Malley well from being around the Dáil. All private secretaries would have known ministers from being in and out of their offices. The office arrangements were cramped and you'd be told to get out when something important was being discussed. Yet we were privy to a lot of important information even though we were on the lowest rung of the ladder. I got on very well with George Colley and hoped he would stay in Education. He was passionate about education long before he entered politics. He was organised and knew his brief.

'My understanding is that Colley told Lemass, "I'm not moving from Education unless I agree to my successor." A number of names were rejected until Donogh was mentioned and Colley said yes. I was uneasy about O'Malley's pending takeover but George allayed my fears:

"Look, he'll drive the department mad, but he'll be brilliant. He's his own man and it will be difficult to control him."

'The best advice I got was from his ex-private secretary in Health: "Stand up to him. If he says to you, 'I Fucking told you to do this,' You must be firm and reply, 'You fucking didn't tell me,' and you'll be fine."

'That's exactly how we got on. If he saw fear, especially in senior civil servants, he'd definitely put the boot in. He loved to get people on the run. Occasionally he'd roar at me. "Did you not ring fuckin' [Arthur] Gibney yet?" And I'd reply, "Will you gimme an effing chance to dial the number."

'He really settled down quite quickly, and he was very well liked in the department. He had scant interest in detail and minutiae. It was the big stroke always. He certainly gave the senior civil servants great encouragement. The whole educational thing was flying and it was a time of great change. He got on very well with Seán Mac Gearailt, the department secretary, a real cute Kerryman from Ardfert. They had a father-and-son relationship.

'Departments love to have strong ministers because they feel they will fight for them at the Cabinet table. Free education got us all excited. Every speech he made was getting headlines and the department loved that. It bolstered our place in the pecking order and Education was regarded as a vibrant place to work.

'He was always up for a bit of craic when you least expected it. He'd say about Lemass for instance, "How could you work with a hoor like that." In truth Lemass was fond of him although it would be difficult to envisage Donogh sitting at one of those poker games with him. They read each other quite well, though. Donogh would try to cut corners and Lemass went along up to a point. Lemass allowed him to go ahead with his announcement of free education on the most oblique of approvals. Donogh was a little more intimidated by de Valera – "the long fucker," as he was wont to refer to him.'

O'Dalaigh got married a few months after O'Malley took over Education and for the first time saw the drawing power of the minister.

'Donogh and Hilda came to the wedding. He had just announced the free education policy and he was the man of the moment. He was hugely newsy and the media were all over the place. We made the evening papers, pictured with Donogh and Hilda. His understanding and manipulation of the media was comprehensive. He read newspapers like a glutton eats food. He'd read the early edition, the later edition and used the media very well.

'He passed on details about events to John Healy in particular. I wouldn't have been aware of what he was leaking to him, but he clearly was, much to the annoyance of Lemass at times. But Charlie and the others would have been doing it too when it suited them.

O'Dalaigh recalls a more thoughtful, giving man:

'Donogh was very generous. Very few ministers gave their staff presents at Christmas. He always did. He gave me a real nice shirt (which I keep in a wardrobe). I could tell it was tasteful, expensive. Everybody in the department received a thoughtful and invariably expensive gift. He seemed not to be short of money and rented a roomy apartment on Eglinton

Road, one of the most expensive roads in Dublin.

'Donogh was very assiduous about going home on weekends to be with his family. Even though his weekends were always packed with invitations and such, he made time for the family and he would head to Thomond Park if there was a good match on. He didn't have as many clinics as some of the rural TDs, but then people could go up to him on the street without any bother. They would meet him at the greyhound track and he would invariably have a few bob or a ten-shilling note to pass on.'

O'Malley was not without his peculiarities, especially when it came to driving: 'He always sat in the front seat even though he was a very nervous passenger. I travelled with him a few times, and Tom Hanahoe, his driver, (a great friend of mine still) would say to me as we were heading down the country: "Watch now when I put on the speed." Donogh would be reading the paper as the car picked up speed: 30, 40, 50. When we hit the open road Tom would put the boot down and we'd be at 70. "Jesus, Tom, you'll fuckin' kill us all!" If Donogh knew the area well, say in his constituency, and we came to a bad bend, he'd catch the strap in terror. It was amazing.

'He'd get back at us in other ways, though. Sometimes when we were driving he'd be fiddling with the radio knob. He knew that Tom and I were passionate about classical music. He'd tune into an aria or some operatic piece and say, "Isn't that your music, boys?" knowing damn well it was, whereupon he'd promptly turn it off. He'd be a terrible messer like that and he'd delight in our reaction.

'Outside of family, politics was his life. There was no time for reading, listening to music, film-going. He didn't seem to be interested in the social whirl that much. He was an immaculate dresser – he was voted the second-best dressed man in Ireland one year. No doubt Hilda made sure he was well turned out. He would often decline dinner functions at night.

'His eating habits were abstemious. At official dinners he wouldn't have soup, for instance, or dessert. He would have fresh salad, fruit juice. This deliberation was out of necessity. I had seen ministers come in at twelve stone and two years later they weighed fourteen stone and more after a succession of functions and dinners.

'More than anything I think he loved to talk politics, be it with Charlie, Brian, John Healy or Arthur Gibney. He enjoyed meeting his close friends at restaurants and the rapport was good through all the mischief and the banter. Healy spent many a late hour in his flat talking politics.' O'Malley and Brian Lenihan had a common interest in soccer. He also had a high regard for Jock Haughey, Charlie's brother, who won an All-Ireland football medal with Dublin in 1958.

O'Dalaigh appreciated the theatrical dimension that Donogh indulged in when occasion demanded: 'When he was in total command of his brief he would discard his notes with a flourish in the midst of a heated debate and improvise. This was quite dramatic really and he was brilliant. But he'd have known the subject thoroughly and wouldn't stray from the issue.

'There's no doubt in my mind where his son Daragh got his theatrical instincts from. Donogh told me that from the earliest days the boy wanted to perform. He wanted the garage of the home converted into a little theatre. Donogh cultivated the boy's love of acting. He asked my advice about buying lighting and props. We went to Burkes Electric and bought a few lamps. These were set up in the garage for a play young Daragh was doing with the neighbouring kids. He got the acting bug early and he has been quite successful. He's a very strong personality and he plays himself all the time really. He is perhaps best remembered for his performance on the RTÉ series, *Home Ground*.'

Watching his children grow – daughter Suzanne would become an artist – enhanced O'Malley's awareness of the quality of education. He wanted secondary education to be more than merely competent and functional. This candid aspiration was expressed in one of his last speeches, 'Thoughts on Art and Education', made at a meeting in the Ursuline Convent, Waterford in January 1968. The *Irish Independent* described this speech as 'quite sensational':

> It is my conviction that every child should have some formal visual education, be it only a drawing class, and as far as in me lies, I intend to do a great deal about it. There is a latent talent in Ireland such as few other countries possess, but my neglect of the arts and my failure to provide adequately in our schools for music, drama, a knowledge of our national treasures and our wonderful ancient monuments must be put right.

His commitment to the arts in education pointed the way to his successors as ministers for education.

His dreams for a more enlightened GAA were defiantly stated that same month when he opened a rugby pavilion:

Rugby and soccer people are sick and tired of having the finger pointed at them as if they were any worse Irishmen for playing these games. When Ireland was asked for sons to call to the colours we were there and were not asked what shape of a ball we used.

He did not live to see the 'ban' rescinded. Within two months he was dead.

10

'A LITTLE DALLAS'

On the Thursday before he died, Donogh O'Malley made one of his rare live appearances on RTÉ Television. He was a guest of Father Tom Stack on the late night religious programme, *Outlook*. O'Malley spoke about counselling services in primary schools. It was a short programme but the minister was uneasy. 'He was extremely nervous before going live on air,' says Stack. Daragh O'Malley watched the programme from his home in Limerick and thought his father looked unwell – 'ashen', as he described it.

'I didn't notice anything like that,' Stack recalls. 'He was in great form in the make-up room and I remember him telling one of the girls to "Gimme a Number 8. Make me look like Dorian Grey and rid me of the sins of my past."' After the programme they had dinner with Brian Lenihan.

'When he became established in politics, and stayed in Dublin, Donogh had many female admirers. He was a very handsome and athletic man; he was colourful, flamboyant and emotional. He stood out without even trying and I suspect he was well aware of this and played along with it to a certain degree. That was the rogue in him again. He would have been great winding people up – even the ladies – and of course he was liable to tell them everything and anything just for the fun of it.

'There was a quieter side to him. Some say he was lonely; he may have been but not in the conventional way. Truly, he was a bit of a poet and was very sensitive. We had some fairly intense private discussions about religion and the Church especially when he was pushing for the amalgamation of the universities.

'Those who knew him would tell you stories about him, some true, many untrue, but all embellished with each telling, as these things tends to be. There was one story about a speech he gave in St John's Pavilion in Limerick. The only problem was that no one showed up to listen to this speech. So he asked the cleaning woman to sit down on a chair in the hall and spoke directly to her. He had to speak in order for the speech to be recorded and printed.

'He could be very funny and witty at times. I remember one time around Christmas I was going out to purchase a Christmas gift. As I passed the Hibernian Hotel I met Donogh on his way out. He asked me where I was going and he said, 'Come on with me.' In we went to Brown Thomas. I was looking for a handbag for a parishioner. Donogh goes up to the lady in charge and says, 'Give this man the best handbag you have. He's a friend of mine.' Before I could protest, I had purchased a handbag worth £30. That was a lot of money in those days. Donogh was nowhere to be seen.

'I was a curate out in Glendalough when Donogh pushed through his free secondary education. On that Sunday [of his death] in March, the Masses were over, and early in the afternoon I got a phone call from John Healy who was down in Sixmilebridge. We have 'a little Dallas' was how he put it. Donogh was dead. I was shocked; a sense of incredulity and sadness enveloped the entire country. '

10 MARCH 1968

When will you be back in Dublin?
I'll be back on Tuesday.
Memo from Tony O'Dalaigh to Donogh O'Malley,
8 March 1968

(Tony O'Dalaigh, private secretary of Donogh O'Malley was in Cavan when the minister died. His wife was participating in and amateur dramatic festival that weekend.)

There was no warning, no early symptoms, and if he suffered a few chest pains he wasn't one to complain. News of his death sent shock and disbelief around the country. Tony O'Dalaigh was perplexed and mystified by the incongruity of it all:

'He was always full of life and he was volatile. Some days he'd come in and be in great form; other days he might be quiet, restless, his humour would be very black and he'd be quite a handful. Even so, he was like a tiger by the tail.

'I'm convinced that the cholesterol built up and clogged arteries, which killed him He was well off the drink of course. The earlier abuse of the hard stuff may have resulted from tension. He was intense, full of pent-up energy, and his sleeping pattern was erratic and not very restful.'

John Healy, in retrospect, saw portents of death in certain gestures. One of these was when O'Malley gave him his bound copies of the *Dáil Debates* covering his career at Leinster House. Healy viewed him as a man in a hurry because his time was running out. The political correspondent was emotionally distraught after O'Malley's death but, characteristically, he made certain events square with the copy he was writing for

The Irish Times, so his recall is at best unreliable.

One story has it that O'Malley's final words were: 'I should never have given up the fuckin' drink.' This has the hallmark of the enduring mythology and fiction that surfaces when O'Malley is remembered. O'Malley was not anticipating death. Indeed, he told Cormac Liddy, family friend and *Limerick Leader* correspondent, that his long-term ambition was to be President of Ireland, and to breed a few good horses and dogs during his stay at the Phoenix Park residence.

Two days before he died, O'Malley asked Michael Mills, political correspondent of the *Irish Press,* to call up to his room in Leinster House. O'Malley had recently undergone extensive tests at the Mater Hospital and had been told there was no evidence of any serious ailment. 'It was obvious he was not fully assured,' said Mills. 'I was anxious to get back to my work but he kept urging me to sit and talk. He was obviously lonely and worried, but as usual he made jokes and told stories.'

Mills continues: 'I cried when I heard the news. I had grown extremely fond of his ebullient character, and valued the warmth of his friendship and his liberal thinking on so many issues, which was not governed by consideration of tradition or Party outlook.

'He was one of the most charming people I ever met. He was witty, urbane, and a wonderful companion. He loved the company of journalists, and they, in turn, delighted in listening to his many stories about life in Limerick in his student days. He added details to meet the occasion or to heighten the drama. At the same time there was a great innocence about much of his behaviour.'

Mills was a friend in Dublin attuned, like Father Tom

Stack, to the loneliness that beset O'Malley in his final
weeks.

'THE TRUE STORY'

When Hilda O'Malley and Suzanne went on a week-long
break to Rome early in March of 1968, this allowed father
and son to spend time together alone, unusually for that time
of year. It should have been the first of many shared moments
between father and son, man and boy. Perhaps it was the
very ordinariness of a normal week that made its ending so
devastating.

Daragh was looking forward to the rugby international
against Wales on the coming Saturday. His father had made
arrangements for the state car to bring him to Dublin, where
he would meet up with him. On the morning of the match,
father and son ate breakfast at the Shelbourne Hotel.

When they arrived at Lansdowne Road, Donogh had a
ticket for his son to sit next to the actor T.P. McKenna. The
minister was seated in the presidential box. 'That was a special
moment for me,' Daragh recalls. 'My interest in theatre was
fast becoming a passion and my pleasure at sitting beside and
chatting to this hugely accomplished actor was beyond words.
T.P. talked to me about my interest in acting, and gave me
books on various aspects of drama and the theory of method
acting.

'The other highlight of that day was when we were making
our way out of the ground. After the match T.P. and I joined
up with my father, and who did we meet among the exiting
throng but Richard Harris? Harris was close to my father
in his youth, although there was a significant age difference
between the two men. My father used to get Harris into

matches at Thomond Park free by carrying him on the bar of his bicycle. The talk changed from rugby to cinema. Harris told my father that he was very hopeful about making a film on Michael Collins.

"'I don't know if that will ever be made, Dickie," my father said to him.

"'Why is that, Donogh?" asked Harris

"'Because you'll never be able to tell the true story," replied Donogh.

'We headed back to Limerick in the state car. We stopped at a sweet shop in Portlaoise, which was sort of a ritual with my father. He always bought a half-pound of pink and white marshmallows and demolished the lot during the remaining journey to Limerick. Donogh kept telling his driver to 'Drive on, can't you', clearly in a hurry to make the first greyhound race at the Markets Field. After the dogs were finished, he headed for the Brazen Head and held court until the small hours. I had a soccer match the next morning, playing for Wembley Rovers against Pike Rovers in Caledonian Park so, after watching some television, I felt tired and headed for bed.

'The next morning my father was going out to Sixmilebridge in County Clare on a canvas and to speak after Mass on behalf of Fianna Fáil candidate Sylvester Barrett. From the doorway of my bedroom, he asked if I wanted to go with him but I told him about my match and I said I was also hoping to go to the Markets Field in the afternoon to watch Limerick play St Patrick's Athletic. 'I'll see you tonight so,' he said. He told me he would pick up my mother and sister from Shannon Airport as they were due to land at 2.20. Donogh said he was going to drive straight to the airport from Sixmilebridge. That was the last time we spoke.

'Just after 2pm *Cork Examiner* journalist Arthur Quinlan knocked on the door at Sunville to tell me that my father had been taken ill and was in St John's Hospital. There would be no soccer match for me that afternoon. When I got to the hospital I sat with my grandmother, who had arrived before me. Contrary to what has been widely stated, my father wasn't dead when he got to the hospital. In fact he was able to walk into the hospital. He got a second heart attack inside the hospital from which he never recovered. One of the doctors came out to us and said, "I'm so sorry. Donogh has died. We couldn't save him."

'When my mother and sister landed in Shannon they were in for a major shock: there was the unlikely presence of Des O'Malley to meet them and tell them what had happened.'

'The Opposition Are Silent'

Tom O'Donnell remembers that March Sunday: 'My last contact with Donogh was on a Sunday morning in March 1968. He and I were campaigning in a by-election in County Clare. As part of our remit, we were assigned to address constituents in the adjoining areas of Clare. My itinerary took me to Parteen and Clonlara. We were both operating in similar areas.

'I was going by car from one Mass to another and I came upon this small wayside church near Sixmilebridge. I was making good time so I pulled up to listen to Donogh. When he got exercised about something or other his speeches had an effortless tempo. He was at his best in those situations and that Sunday morning he was flying. I can remember it as if it was only yesterday.

'"They said I couldn't get the buses. They said I couldn't get the teachers. They said I wouldn't be able to get the classroom accommodation."

'He paused for a few moments. He was clearly working the crowd.

"'Well, I've got the teachers. The buses are running and we have the accommodation. The education scheme is working, and –" he paused briefly "– The Opposition are silent." It was a command performance. These were the last words I heard him speak.

'I waved and nodded to him as I drove away. Two hours later I was back in Limerick going into Cruises Hotel for a bite of lunch before going back out on a door-to-door canvass in that area.

'I went in the door of the hotel and was informed that Donogh had died. I telephoned the matron at St John's Hospital and my worst fears were confirmed. "It's true, Tom," the Matron told me. "Lord have mercy on his soul."

'She told me to keep it quiet for the time being. "We can't broadcast it yet because his wife (Hilda) is airborne, on the way home from Rome."'

'So that was it. The biggest shock I ever got in my life.'

'Is There any Chance?'
Desmond O'Malley has clear memories of that Sunday in March 1969: 'I was up visiting his mother (my grandmother) that Sunday morning; it was a weekly routine and I'd get the 12:00pm Mass in the Crescent. When I was there the phone rang. She asked me to go out and answer it. It was someone to tell me that Donogh had got a heart attack out in Sixmilebridge and that he was in an ambulance on his way to St John's Hospital. They asked me if I would tell his mother.

She was nearly eighty-eight at the time. It was very difficult to tell her. Joe, her other son, Donogh's brother, was in the house at the time.

'I said I'd go down to St John's and come back with any news. But she insisted on going down with me, even though I tried to persuade her against it. When we got to the hospital, people were already beginning to gather. Presumably word was getting around. Once inside the hospital I got somebody to look after her; I didn't want her to go up to the room where they had taken Donogh.

'After settling her I went up the stairs and headed for the room. There were three doctors with Donogh. They had taken him out of the bed and had him on the floor trying to get his heart restarted. They stayed at it for a good half-hour. I can remember the sweat pouring off at least one of them. They didn't have the equipment back then of course so it was quite strenuous, using their hands pounding and pressing on the chest to bring him back.

'One of the doctors looked up at me and sort of shook his head, and I said, "Is there any chance?" The answer was more or less no and five minutes later they stopped. He was dead.

'My grandmother was a very philosophical woman. She'd lost a number of children prior to that, and her husband died in 1933.'

Was Donogh among her favourites?

'Who can say? She was a very tolerant woman and turned a blind eye to some things. She liked to think that certain things weren't happening when they obviously were.'

THE FUNERAL

Donogh O'Malley was given a state funeral. Lemass and de Valera were in attendance. The tricolour-draped coffin was carried from St John's Cathedral up Mulgrave Street, with the Markets Field, home of Limerick soccer, on the left – home also to Donogh's beloved greyhound track. To the right was St Joseph's Psychiatric Hospital, where Hilda would practise after finishing her internship.

The schools were closed and the thousands of children present added to the sense of innocence and awe. Adults cried unashamedly. The quiet dignified Cork hurling legend Jack Lynch was there in his capacity as Taoiseach, but on a personal level paying respect to a fellow Munster sportsman. O'Malley had incensed Lynch, then Minister for Finance, when he introduced the free education scheme without consulting him. But Lynch, ever the team player in sport and in politics, did not hold grudges.

Archbishop McQuaid was not at the funeral. He never forgave O'Malley for the way he got the better of him in bringing in free secondary education. He had no option but to acquiesce after O'Malley met Cardinal Conway. That kind of loss of control infuriated McQuaid, and he was further angered when O'Malley announced that the government would establish by law one multi-denominational university of Dublin based on a merger of Trinity College and UCD. The minister had not consulted the Churches and this was adding insult to injury. O'Malley was effectively telling McQuaid that the arguments banning Catholic attendance at Trinity were obsolete and out of touch with reality.

The Apostolic Nuncio. Dr Joseph McGeough, was in attendance, and McQuaid's absence came as no surprise.

Even in death, O'Malley trumped the Archbishop.

For Tony O'Dalaigh, still in a state of disbelief, the funeral in Limerick is a blur. 'Of course all the department was down in Limerick. Coming back to Dublin was even worse. I got a fierce sense of melancholy and shock back in the department. It was lifeless. The energy was gone. We didn't get a minister for two months as Jack Lynch took over Education.

'There was a great sense of desolation. You'd be looking for him everywhere, expecting to hear him shouting or charging into the office – papers flying, effing and blinding – only to be met with silence. He didn't even see out his full term with us. He was with us from the autumn of 1966 to March of 1968 – twenty months.

'Eventually Brian [Lenihan] took over. Brian was a lovely man but he'd drive you mad because he kept saying yes to everybody and you'd have to try and pick up the pieces. And then he'd come back after the weekend with bits and pieces written on the back of matchboxes or cigarette boxes, requests from his constituents. I'd be trying to decipher the whole thing.

'I suppose it helped us in the department that he was close to Donogh. I can't envisage anybody else having taken over then. All in all it was a traumatic time and with Brian you had to be on your toes. He'd be due down the country for a meeting and nowhere near ready to go and I'd be urging him on, saying, "Brian, it's five o'clock. You have to be in Sligo at eight. Will you get into the bleedin' car." Of course he took it all in his stride, cool as a breeze. He was great that way.

11

Broken Dreams

'When everything that ticked has stopped'
                                        Emily Dickinson

The sheltered existence enjoyed by Donogh O'Malley's two children ended tragically with the sudden death of their father in 1968, a death that defined and shaped the lives of mother and children.

Daragh, aged fourteen, was unable to grasp the magnitude of the loss. It didn't seem to matter where they went, whether one thing happened more than another. It seemed to matter less and less. Everything changed, out of his control, moving remorselessly forward with every passing moment. When Donogh died, the life in Limerick that was lovingly nurtured died with him and it would never be the same for any of the family

A quietness had come into Sunville House, a silence that wasn't silence at all. Daragh had little desire left for anything in Limerick: there was nowhere he wanted to go; the people he wanted to talk to had grown fewer and fewer. No matter how keenly he ventured in a new direction, it could only take him to the next day. He had to leave. Forty years on, the son is still questioning, remembering and trying to make sense of it all.

One cannot grieve if one cannot love; it is life at its most raw, revealing our fundamental vulnerability and frailty, and our strength and capacity to go on. Living inevitably brings the experience of loss and the suffering that loss bestows. For many, loss and suffering take the form of loneliness before the solace of solitude is understood. To write about it is to diminish it; words are inadequate.

Grief is especially complicated when death is sudden: a last conversation; things left unsaid; images and memories. For Daragh O'Malley the years have not obliterated the memory, although they may have softened the heart's needle of pain.

'When my father died it's true that all that was left in his name were two greyhounds – one called "Silk Socks" and the other "Pride of the Mob" – and a prize bond. Our family was, however, well provided for – my father had seen to that – despite the fact that he had no life insurance. Quite a lot of family assets were in Hilda's name. There was no mortgage to be paid on Sunville House and there were bank shares and houses and land. Even so, there were massive debts to be paid and my mother did pay them almost immediately, sometimes acting on poor advice.

'The most pressing financial obligation was an overdraft given to my father by the Munster and Leinster Bank in William Street, Limerick. The last statement on this account showed an overdrawn amount of £38,267/7s/8d. My mother settled it quickly, and there were no repercussions.

So my father didn't die penniless; we were far from impoverished. My mother was able to buy a house on Rose's Avenue, just off the Ennis Road. And she paid for myself and Suzanne to go to college in the Sorbonne and London respectively. When she ran as an Independent candidate in the 1969 general election, she financed a lavish campaign out of her own funds.

THOSE WINTER SUNDAYS

> Sundays too my father got up early
> and put his clothes on in the blueblack cold,
> then with cracked hands that ached
> from labor in the weekday weather made
> banked fires blaze. No one ever thanked him.
>
> Robert Hayden (1913–80)

'I can hear him still, my father, all the anger and the passion about the people without a chance in life… "and the people of Limerick will not have to go to Camden town."

'Why did it take so long for him to find his right place, and why when he seemed to find these things would they all be so fleeting?

'I see him standing there and I realise he is no longer there. "God protect me from amateurs," a favourite incantation. He is, as he has always been, distant yet close. I feel the questions and I feel the pain that they caused him and I know his questions are mine. His struggle is my own.

'And my mother, her mind racing in west Kerry Irish, knowing more than she would ever say. "It's not what you have, Donogh, that's important, it's who you have."

'I see them both now, chatting, laughing too in animated conversation. "I'll tell you a good one about Ollie the Owl…" Donogh beginning yet another hilarious story about Brian Lenihan, a man he loved. And the ceaseless smoking of cigarettes, sixty to eighty Peter Stuyvesant a day, thinking they were less harmful than the Gold Flake.

'And the radio on a Saturday tuned to the horse racing on the BBC World Service, with commentaries from Peter O'Sullivan at Newmarket and Peter Bromley at Redcar. I can see him waiting to hear the result of a race, backing losers, backing the odd winner but total exasperation when the connection faded or interference drowned a race out. Another call to bookmaker Malachy Skelly: "Hello Eileen, It's DOM I will have three hundred schillings on the last favourite at Redcar." The use of the word "schillings" was for my benefit but I had broken the betting code at an early age.

'Outside the family he was Dunnick the gambler, the drinker, quixotic. In defining himself he would have used the words husband, father, friend. Yet in conversation and interviews he performed a kind of obeisance to politics. For my father, politics was play, the highest of all human pursuits. Play needs no justification. It is the thing itself, the laboratory of all creativity, the chance for greatness.

'After the election [of 1969] my mother returned to medicine. She took up a position at St Joseph's Mental Hospital in Mulgrave Street, and she found her work there very satisfying. Hilda O'Malley died in 1991 at Vincent's Hospital in Dublin. At the end she slipped into a coma and died quietly. She was buried in Limerick on a cold and windy day, joining my father in Mount St Lawrence.

'On the morning of her burial, Taoiseach Charles Haughey read "On Raglan Road", the poem that Paddy Kavanagh had written about Hilda O'Malley, into the record of the Dáil.'

With an inherited Kerry madness and Limerick reckless-

'The Scourge of the Mill Road'.

ensive Donogh O'Malley.

Donogh O'Malley at a social occasion in Limerick.

Donogh and 'Old Dessie' at the wedding of Desmond O'Malley.

Donogh O'Malley, Mayor of Limerick.

The Chief pays tribute to the Prince of Thomond.

Donogh O'Malley with Éamon de Valera and Seán Lemass.

Top: Suzanne, Hilda and Daragh O'Malley beside President de Valera during the funeral Mass in St John's Cathedral.
Bottom: Paddy Hillery and Kevin Boland are among those who carry the coffin.

Daragh O'Malley at his father's funeral.

Part of the huge crowd that attended Donogh O'Malley's funeral.

ness, Daragh is content with the person he has become. His acting career, which began at the London Academy of Dramatic Art, hasn't brought him the acclaim achieved by his contemporaries and friends, Liam Neeson and Pierce Brosnan, but Daragh has worked consistently in film and television and for fifteen years appeared as the co-lead with Seán Bean in *Sharpe*, a Napoleonic saga, which is one of the most successful UK televisions shows of all time.

12

After Donogh: Filling the Gap

'Limerick may never be the same,' concluded the *Limerick Leader* editorial. The gap left by O'Malley would never be filled. For Fianna Fáil, his death revealed the vulnerable state of the Party in Limerick East. His seat had to be retained at all costs. When Hilda refused to go forward (to the delight of a Fianna Fáil rump in the city) Desmond O'Malley filled the vacancy.

Desmond Takes his Uncle's Seat

Desmond was never going to gain popular acceptance in Limerick. He was the opposite of his uncle in many respects. Reared in a quietly cultured family out in Corbally, Desmond was born into the family law practice and Fianna Fáil. In the home, books and politics dominated the conversation.

It was always going to be difficult for Desmond, and it was inevitable that he would lose popular affection in his native city. His father, also called Desmond, and two of his uncles, Michael and Donogh, had served as mayors of the city. Des senior was a highly regarded member of Fianna Fáil but had never been interested in contesting a Dáil election. Seán Lemass valued his input and spoke to him on a regular basis. Éamon de Valera was a visitor to his house. Other visitors included the writer Frank O'Connor, and Gerry O'Brien, brother of novelist Kate O'Brien.

Desmond junior was very active in Fianna Fáil at UCD, but he had no notion of entering a political career. Donogh held the role as full-time politician in the family. Compared to his uncle, Desmond was seen as aloof and snobbish. He would never have been regarded as 'fierce Limerick'. He liked to take part in readings of *Ulysses*, whereas Donogh was more likely to be heard belting out a verse of the Dubliners hit song 'Seven Drunken Nights' (1967). His children were enthusiastic about *Top of the Pops* and they probably relegated Ronnie Drew to second place behind the likes of Cliff Richard.

Des O'Malley qualified as a solicitor in 1962, and took over his father's practice when he died in 1965, after playing a lesser role in the practice for some time because of ill-health. Desmond was twenty-nine when his uncle died. He had married a friend of his college days, Pat McAleer of Omagh, and they had three young children. Though he may have been the obvious choice for Fianna Fáil, it was not an easy decision to give up a lucrative and secure legal practice for a risky life in politics.

In the 1969 general election Hilda O'Malley ran as an Independent after being snubbed by Fianna Fáil. This left Desmond with a fight on his hands and Neil Blaney and his activists headed to Limerick to ensure that the seat was retained for Fianna Fáil. It was a dirty and hard-fought campaign. Blaney saw to that. The Fianna Fáil vote dropped by almost 2,500. The attitude of the Party towards Hilda O'Malley showed a great lack of sensitivity. Charlie Haughey, who had been close to Donogh, turned his back on her.

Fine Gael's Tom O'Donnell topped the poll for the first time ever, and would never thereafter be less than dominant in Limerick East. Desmond was elected, but only just, benefitting from Jim O'Higgins's transfers. Fianna Fáil had lost their dominant position in Limerick East. At the count, held in the School of Commerce, Dessie was observed sitting alone in his car, crestfallen. His wife Pat tried to have him mingle with the Party activists in the school but to no avail. What his thoughts were at this time may never be known. He had defeated Labour's Mick Lipper by a mere 900 votes.

The 1969 election only accelerated the inevitable; O'Donnell, with the help of his political machine in Bruff, would have topped the poll in 1973 anyway.

Times had certainly changed.

'Rory, take the seat, you're entitled to it,' O'Malley is supposed to have said to Rory Liddy in his dying moments. Liddy, who twice served as Mayor of Limerick (1958–9 and 1970–1), travelled everywhere with his friend; they were like brothers. Liddy was the first to get to Donogh when he collapsed, and went with him to the hospital. It was a devastating ending to a lifelong friendship.

According to Desmond:

> I didn't really foresee myself spending a lot of time in politics. They were really only pushing me to go and stand for the by-election because they felt I had a better chance of winning it than anyone else. And I thought I might be released out of the situation when the next general election came around.

But by that time everyone seemed to take it absolutely for granted that I would stay on. And I suppose to some extent that I got a taste for it by that stage as well. I decided I would stay because I had committed myself and I had a certain obligation to stay at that stage. I could not give it up, even though quite honestly, when I did stand the first time I envisaged being there for maybe a year or two.

Hilda O'Malley didn't see it quite like that. 'They have short memories,' was her icy comment. Hilda O'Malley was not cut out for politics. She felt herself obliged to run for election to save her husband's seat. The bad blood that ensued between herself and Dessie lingered. Fianna Fáil emerged from this episode with little distinction.

Desmond's late father would not have allowed this scenario to unfold. A seat in the Senate for Hilda would have been an appropriate gesture. In their urgency to retain the Dáil seat at all costs Fianna Fáil was found wanting. Desmond had got a taste for politics and his political ambitions took precedence. Perhaps some of these thoughts were running through his mind when the votes were being counted.

There was resentment that he was stepping in the considerable shadow of Donogh. Twenty years later the resentment surfaced again when Dessie had made his own imprint on the national political scene, breaking away from Fianna Fáil to found the Progressive Democrats in 1985.

Donogh often said in relation to his nephew: 'That young fella [or 'little bollix' as he sometimes called him] inherited the worst elements of both sides of the family.' It is doubtful whether he would have agreed with him on many issues. Desmond's tenacity, another O'Malley trait, brought unpopularity in Limerick. He had long since lost the affection of his native city.

'Let's Hope He Does Something Constructive'

Daragh O'Malley speaks in refined well-modulated tones. He has long ago come to terms with the death of his father. What he does have is a profound sense of regret over the opportunities squandered by various politicians who were elected in Limerick East after his father died.

In relation to his cousin Desmond O'Malley, who took over the seat from Donogh, Daragh uses football parlance easily and often: 'Dessie was a "penalty kick" to win the seat initially but at important moments in a long political career he kicked for touch when I suppose he should have gone for goal. My mother was not over the moon about the turn of events that saw Des enter politics but she never spoke about Des in a vicious or disparaging way. "Let's hope he does something constructive," she used to say.

'Filling the vacant seat left by my father was problematic for the Fianna Fáil Party. My mother was in a state of shock after the sudden death and loss of her husband; it would take her six months to find some kind of composure. In the meantime she was totally unable to cope with the prospect of taking over Donogh's seat.

'Neil Blaney, the director of elections, felt there was a real danger that the seat might be lost as Party activists in Limerick thought that a lot of Donogh's personal vote would go to Mick Lipper of Labour, including nearly all the soccer vote that my father had so carefully cultivated. The prevailing wisdom indicated that anyone with an O'Malley name would be enough to save the seat.

'Neil Blaney thought otherwise and made an inspired decision by asking perennial candidate Mick Crowe to run. I believe he pledged to finance his campaign, the strategy being that although Crowe wouldn't win he would garner some of the soccer vote that would have otherwise gone to Lipper. After a close call Dessie held the seat, reaching a quota on the eleventh count, with the Crowe vote making all the difference between winning and losing for Mick Lipper. Another master stroke from the skilled tactician Neil Blaney

'When the general election came around Hilda had improved to the point where she now wanted the Fianna Fáil nomination. However, the message from Fianna Fáil headquarters was that Hilda O'Malley was not to be selected at convention. She withdrew from the race before the Party convention.

'This only strengthened Hilda's resolve and she decided to run as an Independent. Neil Blaney thought she had a decent chance of a seat if she used an Independent Fianna Fáil moniker. Hilda was so disgusted with Fianna Fáil that she wanted nothing to do with them. The crucial mistake she made was not going as an Independent Fianna Fáil candidate. This without doubt cost her the election

'I have one vivid memory of that general election campaign and a speech I gave outside Todds with 25,000 people gathered. But the general election of 1969 in Limerick East was a brutal and dirty affair that split families throughout the constituency. The widow of Donogh O'Malley pitted against her nephew. After that election there was virtually no contact between my mother and Des O'Malley until the day she died.

'Nobody Minding the Shop'

'Despite what people might think, I have great personal respect for Des O'Malley. He was by far this State's best ever Minister for Industry and Commerce. I am very sorry he didn't become Taoiseach, The opportunity was there for him, and if he had not followed such bad advice, well, who knows. It would have been nice, I suppose, to see an O'Malley leading the country.

'Des is not the dour individual he appears to be; he is a great comrade on a high stool, he is a major raconteur with a great sense of fun, and as a child I saw him acting in Brandon Thomas's *Charley's Aunt* and Agatha Christie's *Ten Little Indians* on stage for the College Players in Limerick, and he was absolutely brilliant. Des also endears himself to me insofar as he is fond of a bet on the horses and, like a lot of O'Malleys, Des devours cigarettes more than is good for him. I had a few pints recently with him in the Waterloo on Baggot Street, and I thoroughly enjoyed a wonderful evening in his company.

'Donogh, I suppose, would not look too kindly at recent events in his beloved city. I think my father would be horrified if he could see what has happened in Limerick. It's a major stain on several political careers, and it's so sad in many ways. Limerick needed minding but there has been nobody minding the shop for the last three decades. My father and Tom O'Donnell worked long and hard to put the Shannon region on a solid economic footing. Either of them would have put their seats on the line to maintain the status quo in the Shannon-Aer Lingus-Heathrow débâcle. They would have done this because they were selfless people and not self-serving.

'The quality of politician in Ireland is of course at its

lowest in the history of the state. I just can't believe the terrible social problems: the poverty; the drugs; the killings; the unveiling, at a cost to the Irish taxpayer of one billion euro, of vast tracts of political corruption. And then there's the continued impoverishment of the health service; and the renewed apartheid in education.

'The quality of life for the generation in waiting is certainly diminished. I think it is imperative too that Irish people remember who they really are and keep their sense of identity. It's a multicultural society now, but I would hope to see a greater retention and cultivation of things Irish. Maybe I'm being unrealistic, but we should try and remain Irish and perhaps make some belated effort to learn the Irish language. We have lost so much of our identity to a scavenging Celtic Tiger.'

Two Types of Simplicity

In an interview in Dublin in May 2007, as the fortieth anniversary of Donogh's death approached, Desmond O'Malley recalled this turbulent period in his life and career, and evinced a profound sense that he was he more sinned against than sinner in his native city.

> The horror of accusing morning light
> Condemns me to another hideous day.
> Did someone cry? What did I do last night?
> Was someone hurt? Insulted? What did I say?
>   Brendan Kennelly, 'Healer'

He opens his mouth to speak, hesitates and shifts uneasily in the silence. His gaze is fixed on a building site in the distance. Our eyes don't meet even as we speak. Desmond O'Malley's feelings about his uncle are ambiguous. The enmity is lessened, although still profound; the memories, often painful, endure. He answers questions sparingly. The responses are halting, guarded. From silence to silence a partial depiction emerges.

'Hilda told me that I was mad to stand for the vacant seat, and that, particularly, Haughey and Blaney were the two she didn't trust,' he says.

Why did Hilda change her mind the following year?

'I don't know. She seemed to change her tune, although not about Fianna Fáil; she continued to be opposed to them and decided to stand as an Independent candidate.

'The impression was that I had forced my way in against her wishes the previous year. This amazed me and a lot of people because she held the opposite view. Living up to the image of Donogh was a problem at the time and this didn't help in any way.'

His relationship with the more charismatic uncle might best be described as strained.

'He was very unpredictable and rather difficult when he had drink taken, at least for the family members. My father had to devote a lot of time to bailing him out of various drunken escapades and difficulties he got into. He found it very hard to get de Valera to look a bit more kindly on him. De Valera was not impressed with him at all. Lemass, fortunately for Donogh, was more amenable. De Valera wouldn't appoint him to anything and didn't.

'Lemass was prepared to take risks with him, if you like, and my father was in a better position to talk to Lemass; he knew the two of them quite well. Lemass was more understanding of human frailties certainly. I think that's why Donogh was appointed. My father promised Lemass he would keep an eye on Donogh, and in fairness, he did calm down a lot. Lemass took a calculated gamble and it paid off. Dev wasn't prepared to take those risks.

'He wasn't in government long enough to assess him as a politician. He was forty-seven when he died; he was in the Dáil for fourteen years. The early years were a bit wild. George Colley and Paddy Hillery, especially, had a lot of the groundwork done in regard to the free education. Donogh got all the credit.' He laughs wryly. 'Jack Lynch [Minister for Finance] was out of the country when the announcement was made, and he was quite annoyed. He had to find the money to pay for it.'

'I did not get along terribly well with Donogh. My father had a lot of problems with him. Then after he became ill I was left to pick up some of the pieces, to try and sort out some of the mess. Donogh wasn't very helpful. He didn't take account of the effect he was having on other people, and the damage he was doing to them. As I said, I found it difficult to deal with him.'

The subject is closed; Desmond's gaze remains fixed on the window and once more silence prevails.

The interview continues with questions about the events after his uncle's death. 'I wasn't very keen to step into the breach because I had a good practice. Within a very short time, I got stuck with the Arms Crisis. I suppose that couldn't have been foreseen, but it turned out to be very difficult.'

He dismisses the notion that Donogh might have been Taoiseach material. 'Who can say, he might have been, but I don't think he would have. He'd have wanted it all right. He had a fairly colourful career which might not have suited a lot of people.'

He doesn't speak with any great conviction about the

relationship between Donogh and Charlie Haughey. 'I feel he was relatively close to Haughey and he might have gone along with some of the stuff that Haughey and those were venturing into. Donogh wasn't a great money manager and it's conceivable that he would have got heavily into debt because of his generosity. This might have given Haughey leverage over him financially. He was inclined to spend a lot of money that he didn't have, and that might have influenced how the situation played out.'

The interview is finished and a few idle moments pass while he goes into the bedroom to talk to his wife, Pat. There is a well stocked library on one wall – political biographies, literature and poetry, including a well-thumbed copy of Patrick Kavanagh's *Collected Poems*.

Kavanagh is one of his many favourites – Frank O'Connor, Sean O'Faolain, and many others are mentioned. 'Kavanagh's is a book one dips into on occasion,' he says. 'The story behind "Raglan Road" has been well documented. I think Kavanagh was a bit of a nuisance really. Certainly Donogh wasn't threatened by his hovering in the background. Did he love Hilda or was he in love with the idea of loving her?' With that he goes to the three poems entitled 'Hilda.' He becomes animated momentarily but then the book is put back.

The visitor asks to see some pictures of Donogh. There is only the one, on display with all the others. It's a photograph of Donogh and Desmond senior taken on Desmond's wedding day. They are dressed in formal attire but in the picture both men are relaxed and smiling.

'If you look closely,' Desmond says, 'you can see that they each have a cigarette in their hand. It's hardly a surprise that they both died relatively young,' he says, fumbling to light his own cigarette. If he is aware of the irony, it doesn't penetrate the silence. The cigarette remains unlighted.

Patrick Kavanagh once said that there are two types of simplicity – the simplicity of going and the simplicity of return, the latter being the ultimate in sophistication. Desmond O'Malley is now back in Dublin. What he thinks, what he feels and sees around him is anyone's guess.

13

A Proud Republican of the Old School

Paddy Kiely, former Mayor of Limerick, lives at 6 Pennywell Avenue, a modest terraced house. The entrance is on Keating Avenue, around the corner. This is the heart of old Limerick, dominated by the spire of St John's Cathedral. Paddy has lived in this house for the greater part of his life, and raised his family there. Grandchildren are playing in another room.

Not a lot has changed in the immediate locality apart from the constant traffic at the lights where Clare Street intersects with Pennywell. Even so, much has been lost, the salient thing being the decline of simplicity. In the 1930s and 1940s, Pennywell had the sense of a little village with St Patrick's Church, three pubs, a post office, five sweet shops and the Good Shepherd laundry. Two hurling teams, St Patrick's and Claughaun, drew from the neighbourhood. The church and post office are still there but gone is the sense of community.

Paddy Kiely is an O'Malley man through and through. O'Malley was a frequent visitor to the house and it was here that Paddy got to know him and his elder brother Desmond. His recollection and assessment may be biased but his loyalty to the family is unwavering. He points to a rare print of the men who died in the 1916 Rising. 'I picked that up for 2/6d in the market many years ago, and I was offered two hundred quid for it at one point. I wouldn't sell it,' he says. He is a proud republican of the old school and a bit bewildered by recent events in the North. 'What did they fight for?' he asks, not wanting an answer.

'I first met Donogh around 1948, just casually. Donogh became the third O'Malley brother to hold the office of Mayor. [Donogh served as Mayor for six months only, June –December 1961; he resigned from the position on being appointed Parliamentary Secretary to the Minister for Finance.] I was mixed up in his political career since 1952. He went before the Fianna Fáil convention in 1952 and was beaten. Two years later [1954] he won the convention by six votes, defeating J.C. Duggan, who was President of the Insurance Institute of Limerick in 1946-7. J.C. worked for Sun Life of Canada in those days.'

This was a tentative beginning to O'Malley's political career, a fact not lost on Kiely: ''Twas a lucky day for Limerick that Donogh got the convention. He came that close to not getting it.'

Kiely's recollection reveals the best and worst tendencies that fuelled O'Malley's drive. He was no revolutionary, temperamentally or otherwise, but, as Kiely indicates, he worked his constituency carefully, he understood the value of good press relations, and most important, he never missed a chance to promote the interests of his native Limerick, and made sure that he was seen to get the credit for it.

Kiely was well aware of O'Malley's drinking binges and the dangers inherent in them. He was tempestuous and unpredictable and violent. It was no surprise that Party leaders were frightened of him and his undisciplined episodes. There was a real fear that he might undermine Party cohesion and a considerable doubt about his ability to work within a team.

When the count was taking place during the 1954 election, Kiely and his friend Seán O'Malley were in and out of the courthouse checking for an update or a result. It was three in the morning before O'Malley was elected, but Kiely was not to know that.

'Myself and Seán were met outside the courthouse by old Dessie and he said that Donogh was beaten. We left the courthouse and went up O'Connell Street crying. At the time we were only young fellas. Anyway, we emptied our pockets and went over to the Hazel and had a feed. We came back down to the courthouse, not knowing what to do with ourselves, and there was the bould Dessie outside bursting his sides laughing.

'"Ye took me serious," says he.

'We did of course.

'"Well, he's elected now."

Kiely laughs at the memory: ''Twas only like yesterday, 'tis so clear in my mind. Feckin' Dessie caught us good, though, right enough.'

Kiely worked closely with Donogh, and the following year [1955] Donogh was elected to the Limerick Corporation as an alderman. He was on the city council until December 1961, when he had to retire due to his appointment by Seán Lemass as Parliamentary Secretary to the Minister for Finance.

O'Malley's appointment to the Cabinet as Minister for Health, in 1965, was received with huge excitement in Limerick. 'The night he came back to Limerick,' Kiely recalls, 'he was escorted from the cross of Pennywell and Clare Street to the Monument in O'Connell Street, where he addressed the public.

'When the speech-making was over we went around all the corporation housing estates meeting people, shaking hands. 'Twas a very long night, and we didn't finish until early on Saturday morning. But that was Donogh. He wouldn't stop until he was satisfied that he'd met them all. And feck it if he wasn't still full of energy. We were knackered but he was flying it still.'

Kiely witnessed Donogh's interest in education a decade before he delivered on free secondary schooling. 'When Donogh became Minster for Education they'll tell you that the rest is history. That may well be but I can tell you that he was drawn to education long before that and I remember a promise he made to a bunch of young fellas here in Limerick in 1957.

'There was a crowd of us down in the election rooms and we were packing up stuff. At two in the morning Donogh knocked on the door. "What are ye doin' here at this hour of the morning,' says he. 'In the name of Jaysus let the boys go home to bed." We were nearly finished at that point so Donogh told us to wait till he came back. Off he went down to the Coliseum Café and he came back with fish and chips for everyone.

'He went around talking to all the young fellas.

'"When did you lave school?"

'"What certificate have you?"

'"Have you the Primary or the Inter?"

'He was going along like that asking the same questions. Then he came to this fella, Jack O'Reilly [now deceased].

'"Why didn't you stay at school?"

'Jack replied straight into his kisser: "Because my parents couldn't afford to keep me to go to school."

138

'Donogh said no more. He sat down without a word. After about five minutes he got up.

'"Lads,' says he, "if I ever become Minister for Education, I'll straighten out that problem fairly quick."

'That was the beginning of his interest in education. I told that story off of St Michael's altar on the day Jack O'Reilly was being buried. Fr Donogh O'Malley [distant relative] who said the Mass, was very surprised upon hearing this. And why wouldn't he. Sure no one else knew about it.'

Rows, Disagreements and Making Up

'We would have several rows on the running of Fianna Fáil. I had a bit of a set-to with him several weeks before he died. My mother was sick at the time. He was mad to make it up with people. He came out of the Brazen Head pub and crossed O'Connell Street. I was standing outside Clancys [electric shop] and he approached me.

'"How's your mother, Paddy?"

'"Well, Donogh, she can't be too good after two heart attacks and the accident, as you know. But I think she'll survive."

'Next thing he started shivering.

'"Is there something wrong with you too?" says I. "You'd want to look after yourself. That shivering isn't good."

'"Ah, I'm grand, Paddy."

'This encounter took place less than a month before O'Malley died.

'He died on the afternoon of my birthday. But worse still, I had to go down into Barrington's Hospital and tell my mother that he was dead. She burst out crying.

'What she always liked to say about him was: "There's a

man that you could fight with but he'd always make it up with you." That was one of the reasons he was so popular and loved by the working-class people of Limerick.

'You could expect anything to come out of his mouth. His motto was: "In politics you must be able to genuflect in front of bishops, put on the right coat to go down to St Mary's Park, and then go out to the fuckin' snobs on the Ennis Road with the right coat as well, and a little bit of a twang."

'There was one election campaign and we were canvassing in Mayorstone Park. We weren't there long when Donogh says, "Come on away out of this feckin' place, we're getting nothing here.' We headed down to Mary's Park to continue the canvass. We were going well and the reaction was good until he met someone from Mayorstone Park who said, "We voted for you, Donogh."

'Well, he turned on the man and let fly. "Listen," he said. 'I got more votes out of Mary's Park than I ever got in Mayorstone, and the fuckin boxes proved it!" He was deadly like that but he knew his constituency and where his support came from.'

'The Job is Done, Paddy'

'He'd go on batters and word spread quickly when this happened. Those in the know would give him a wide berth and were careful when they approached him. Donogh and myself were after having another row and I sent up a fella to him one morning with a letter. I told the man, "He's on the batter now so be careful. Just give him the letter and see what he has to say. Let me know how you get on."

'The man came back to me later in the day to tell me what happened.

140

'"He says to me, why didn't fuckin' Kiely come up with this himself?"

'"But where did he put the note," I asked him.

"In his top pocket," was the reply.

"Leave it alone so, it's OK."

'That was on a Saturday morning. The following Wednesday the man came back to the shop to me, and says he, "The job is done, Paddy."

'Donogh never asked anybody their politics, or any of the O'Malleys for that matter. If a turn could be done it would be done. Hilda was like that too. She'd go out of her way to help people.

'A memorable confrontation took place when Donogh went in to the Jesuits on a Good Friday. He had no drink taken for several weeks. There was a Jesuit priest who saw this and could and did tell the story better than me.

'Anyway this old snob of a one came up to him and asked him how his mother was.

'"Tis like this now, mam: She's waiting to hear this.

"Donogh falls the first time.

Donogh falls the second time.

Donogh meets his poor afflicted mother.

And would you ever fuck off outta here now!"

'All the priest could do was turn away to hide his laughter.'

Paddy Kiely recalls innumerable instances of O'Malley's generosity. 'When Donogh said he'd do a thing 'twas done. Eddie Donnelly owned a meat shop in Gerald Griffin Street. Donogh used to leave him one thousand pounds a month to make sure that anyone who hadn't got food got it. Shortly after Donogh died, I went into Eddie to collect insurance.

He was telling me about money Donogh gave him. I wasn't inclined to believe him until he showed me the books and all the cheques. The last cheque wasn't lodged.'

14

The Dubliner Who Came To Stay

Jack Bourke was a stalwart in the world of Limerick theatre. The Fianna Fáil member served three terms as Mayor of Limerick and was Chairman of the Mid-Western Health Board for nineteen years.

Bourke arrived in Limerick in the mid-1950s to manage the old Ritz Cinema. With the support of his father, Lorcan Bourke, he converted the cinema into what became the City Theatre. All of the big names of the day appeared in various productions, but the overheads of running the City Theatre, combined with the modest size of the regular theatre-going public, led to its eventual closure. 'Limerick was the best cinema- and theatre-going place in the country before the advent of TV changed everything,' Bourke says.

Jack and his wife Monica (also from Dublin) have been living in their home in Roxboro since 1962. The couple raised four children and have six grandchildren.

Jack Bourke is sitting in the Railway Bar in Limerick.

'I had a very high regard for Donogh. He was larger than life and I often wonder how things would have turned out if he had lived.'

Jack Bourke's initial meeting with O'Malley was

memorable for all the wrong reasons. However, this was in accord with an O'Malley tendency. Bourke may not have known this at the time, but he was being 'measured' by the man who would become his friend.

'I first met him in the Glentworth Hotel, which was sort of the place to be at that stage. Donogh arrived in one Thursday night and asked to meet me – for what reason I don't know. He had just become a minister. Anyway, I went over and met him. My father was Lord Mayor of Dublin at the time.

'He said to me: "You're father made a bollix of the Lord Mayoralty."

'I said, "You're probably a bit of a bollix yourself. What I suggest you do is say that to my father because he's a big man, and he could take care of you any time."

'He got a bit testy.

'"If you want to come around the corner and we'll have this out," I said, "I'm game."

'A few people stepped in, fortunately.

Fortunately for who, though?

'Well, both of us, I'd say. Mind you, I did a lot of boxing and wrestling in my youth, and I was younger and stronger. He spent the rest of the following day chasing around looking for me, to apologise.

'Not too long after that, I was crossing Thomas Street to Bedford Row, and he stops in the state car. He said, "You're going to run for us in the local election."

'I said to him, "Are you effing mad?" And he asked why.

'"I'm from Dublin," I said, "and I'll get two votes, my wife – and I'm not sure she'd vote for me anyway – and myself."

'"That doesn't make any difference. You'll be elected."

'I said, "OK, I'll have a go. Tell me what to do."

'He told me to join a cumann and we'd take it from there. So I joined the local cumann.

'They used to meet down in Frank Glasgow's little shop in Bedford Row. It was a small gents' outfitter beside the Savoy cinema. I was put before the hierarchy there and it went through unanimously. I'm certain Donogh had instructed everybody that it was to be unanimous. To everybody's surprise, including me, I was elected.

'I'm not sure my wife voted for me,' he says mischievously. 'She says she did.'

Jack Bourke was Mayor of Limerick when O'Malley died. His recall of the day is vivid.

'I was in Cappamore speaking outside the church door. The Party played hard with me. Everybody who could speak was expected to do so at all the churches on a Sunday morning. They gave me all the places that had a seven in the morning Mass. So I finished up after the early Mass in Cappamore. Somebody came over to me on my way back to Limerick and said, "Donogh is dead."

'I thought it was some sort of a joke because I had been with him the night before and he seemed to be as healthy as a fish. But he was dead all right. I mean what can you say even now other than that it was tragic. It was an obscenely young age to die. Like many others, I felt his loss acutely. Here was the man that got me into politics and now I had to attend his funeral as Mayor of Limerick. It was the biggest funeral I ever saw…' Bourke's voice trails off and he remains silent for several moments as his mind wanders back to that week in March 1968.

Bourke is a gregarious, yet deeply religious man. He is still regarded in some quarters as a blow-in, even after fifty years. His vivacious and warm personality hides a thoughtful, introspective man. His passion for Dublin football has endured but he doesn't get homesick for the city of his birth. 'Remember,' he says, 'I've spent much more of my life in Limerick than in Dublin.' He is widely read, and although he is not lacking in modesty, his observations are anything but facile. Of Donogh he says:

'He was a great rogue in his own way and he was always up to devilment. You never knew when he was being serious or when he was ball-hopping. The one great memory I have of him is when the question of a university for Limerick was being debated. The push was on in a big way for a university. He eventually told them all to fuck off if they were looking for a traditional university. He maintained that such an institution catered to the professional classes – doctors, lawyers, all the professions that didn't create jobs

'I remember him saying: "This is going to be a technologically-based university. While I'm there in the Department of Education, nobody will change it. That's the way it's going to be."

'Between that and his free education – and very few will admit this – he was the architect of the Celtic Tiger. It took a generation for it to kick in. And there's another point that should be made. Today, the famous or infamous O'Malley Park has over one hundred kids attending the University of Limerick. Very few people know that; indeed many would be astonished to know it.

'These things wouldn't have happened except for Donogh. He had the place picked out [for the National Institute of Higher Education, now the University of Limerick] in Plassey. It was really marvellous foresight; the land was there, the magnificent white house, which is still there. I often think that, historically, he has not been fully acknowledged for his contribution. He is not mentioned in any recent guide-book to Limerick. You'll see the likes of a Richard Harris, a J.P. McManus and a Frank McCourt all lauded. What the fuck any of these people did for Limerick is dubious.

'Donogh, like many of us, was fond of a sup. Once he gave up the drink, he became a different character altogether – very serious and quiet. Before all that, he used to come into our place in Summer Street, where we had Geary's Hotel. He would meet four or five pals and they'd play poker, and many times they'd have a singsong. Donogh had this soprano-type voice, very funny to listen to. He loved to sing and you couldn't stop him once he started. Tom English from Hospital, manager of the Savoy, was a great mate of his; he played a lot of cards with him, as did a fellow called Stewart Klein.

Bourke is somewhat sceptical about many of the so-called stories that affixed themselves to O'Malley, especially in subsequent years. 'You wouldn't call him a saint but by the same token, if he drank and caroused and womanised as stories suggest, he might still be alive. In fact, he would never have made it to high political office. Mind you, none of this mythology is malicious. He was a lovable rogue, I suppose.

'I don't have too many stories about him mainly because he died so young. But there was a couple of events. He used to come out to the captain's dinner in Castletroy Golf Club, himself and Paddy Hillery. Paddy was a keen and very able golfer. They would always finish up playing poker and the steward had great difficulty getting them out of the place at about six in the morning. Donogh knew every little pub in

Limerick where he could go to whenever he wanted to, and he was a great man for staying out till the small hours. He had incredible energy and he could manage on very little sleep.

'Sadly, he was just getting into his stride when he died. I remember being on a deputation to meet him with Limerick Development Association. There was about a half-dozen of us, including Con Shanahan and Denis Nolan, manager of Roches Stores. We met him in his office and he was sitting behind his desk and not a word out of him. He seemed distracted, lost in thought.

'There was a bust of him on the desk. In order to break the silence I asked him who did the bust of him. He snapped out of what seemed like a sleep even though he was awake. Eventually he showed us around the Dáil and the Seanad, and he was his old self.

'"Jack Bourke will be sitting there," he said, pointing to a senate seat. He didn't live long enough to make that happen. I have no doubt he would have wanted me in there. In later years I ran twice for the senate and lost by a vote each time. He would have become leader of the Party. Once he started to behave himself, he was well got with everybody. He was sound as a bell.

'I pointed out how he became a very quiet man, and I think before the end, he was a very lonely man. Contrary to what some might say, giving up the drink isolated him from his drinking pals, and he never got the same kick out of drinking company. Oh he would go to functions and all that but sobriety took some of the spark out of him. But who can say, really? What he was trying to accomplish would have concentrated the mind of any man.

'In the years after free secondary education became reality

it was marvellous to see the people who never thought about education insisting that their kids should get a secondary level education. We had reached the point in Limerick, not too long ago either, where there was 23% unemployment. Today it's virtually a full employment situation. There is heated debate about the numbers of people leaving Dell. It should be pointed out that these are people in the higher echelons of the company, and they want to leave.

'I knew Hilda extremely well. She used to come into our place every morning for coffee. As a student in Dublin in the 1940s, she was stunningly attractive. There was an elegance about her even as she aged. She was a great character, though, and very witty and droll in her own way. She never spoke an awful lot about Donogh but at the same time she never had a bad word to say about him.

'The death of Donogh placed an enormous burden on her and the children. She was very badly treated during the election to fill his seat. She was resilient, however, and went back to finish medicine. I took great pleasure out of receiving her and her daughter and some of her relations in City Hall when I was there. She was a lovely woman.

'The problem with Dessie was you couldn't say anything about him unless it was in praise. Furthermore, he spent too much of his political career trying to step out from the considerable shadow of his uncle. I remember going up to Saint Enda's Hall in Thomas Street for a meeting before the local elections took place. As I was going in I met Dessie at the steps. He said to me, "Jack, do me a favour. Would you ever tell Donogh that I can't run." I asked him if there was any reason he wished to give him and he replied, "No. I don't fucking want to."

'So I went on up before the meeting started. I spotted Donogh and told him I had met Dessie downstairs and gave him the news that Dessie wouldn't be running. "The effin' little bollix," was his reply.

'There were a few choice terms added on but I won't repeat them here. Donogh had made all sorts of bets that Fianna Fáil would have a majority in the City Council, which would be nine seats. And if Dessie had run, we would have got that number. As it was, we got eight seats.

'Donogh had little time for his nephew. Dessie never liked being called 'the Man From Uncle', and he had to take a lot of that during his earlier days. I suppose Donogh was an impossible act to follow and Dessie was keen to make his own name. The fact that he formed his own Party would suggest this. He made his name all right but ultimately, no matter what he achieved, he was always going to be Donogh's nephew.

Bourke rejects the suggestion that O'Malley's money problems left him vulnerable to the influence of Charles J. Haughey. 'At the time of his death, I don't believe Donogh had any money. That's not to say he was without assets. His generosity to those in need of financial help is well documented. To say that Haughey would have owned him financially is nonsense. You'll always get that sort of thing from vindictive individuals trying to blacken his name.'

15

A Blueshirt and Close Friend

Tom English sits erect and alert in the parlour of his O'Connell Avenue home. He is turned out impeccably, in an old-fashioned gentlemanly way. There is an air of dignified civility about this man who has come a long way from his native Hospital. If there is a rough edge to him it is a vestige of his farming, cattle-dealer days.

His voice is strident, punctuated by an occasional cough as he lights a cigar. Outside the front window, little has changed in this locality: the gardens, the hedge and railings and the heavy wrought-iron gate. The house where Donogh O'Malley's mother lived is only a short walk further up the avenue. English speaks wistfully about O'Malley. Forty years on, it is clear that he is missed.

'I socialised with "Dunnick" quite a lot, and he was a fabulous character. When he walked into a crowded room one didn't have to ask who had entered. He had fantastic presence. When he'd be taking a drink, 'twas full-steam ahead. He'd ring me in the morning and we'd go on a tear. There were times when we ended up in the most unusual places, but we spent a lot of time in the Glentworth Hotel, the Brazen Head, and of course Cruises Hotel.

'His idea of a good night out was going to the greyhounds

in Limerick, and then down to Cruises where he'd play cards with Malachy Skelly, Jack Lyons, and a chap called Stewart Klein. We were high-rolling cattle dealers. The game couldn't be big enough for him and we'd often go on until six in the morning.

'There are several stories that I could tell about him and perhaps a few that are better left untouched. One of my favourite memories of him goes back to the time when he was Mayor of Limerick. When he was a made a minister in the government he had to resign as mayor. That was normal procedure but a successor had to be found. At any rate, they coopted a man called Frank Glasgow, a small, very quiet man. He owned a drapers shop in Bedford Row. Moreover, he was a fluent Gaelic speaker with very little charisma.

'Glasgow's first function took place in the clubhouse of Shannon Rowing Club. This was the annual dinner with about 150 people in attendance. Dunnick had already been invited as Mayor and of course he couldn't go in that capacity. He went along in any case even though he was now a minister. That morning Glasgow had received the chain of office.

'It was a smashing occasion and we had a very nice meal. I was sitting with Dunnick and after dinner we headed into the bar. Glasgow may have been overawed by the occasion; he was, shall we say, very nearly inconspicuous. Dunnick headed for the bar and called out to the steward: "Steward. A drink for the house." Whereupon he put up a fifty-pound note.

'"A drink for the house,' he repeated and paused. Then he said, "When I go out for a drink on a Saturday, Glasgow belongs to me!"'

'He was quick-minded like that, and very witty.

'He was back in Cappamore during a by-election and

he gave a speech after Mass. "Well, 'tis true,' he began. "The savage loves his native shore, and I'm delighted to be here among you this morning."

'Two lads listening to this got a bit bothered. "What's he talking about? Is he calling us savages?" And they were ready to attack him, presumably not knowing the old saying. Sure all the O'Malleys originated in Cappamore.

Before O'Malley entered politics, there was concern about his opportunities for employment in Ireland.

'He qualified as an engineer,' English says. 'Joe Griffin, a friend of mine – Griffin Insurances – was one of the few insurance brokers in town at the time. Dunnick was at a loose end at that stage because there was no work for engineers. I remember Griffin telling me that "Old Dessie" [Donogh's elder brother] had said, "If he's not elected, he'll have to go to Canada. I have a single ticket booked for him." But he got in.'

Getting elected kept O'Malley in Ireland and set him on his way to political greatness. English is unequivocal about the reasons for his friend's popularity. 'He was as much at home in St Mary's Park as he was on the Ennis Road. He had a great common touch; if he met you once he remembered who you were.

'I was being interviewed for a job in England not too long after he entered the Dáil, and I gave his name as a reference. During the interview, a letter was produced with the Dáil Éireann letterhead. "I have here a glowing tribute from a member of your parliament," said one of the interviewers. 'Now that didn't do me any harm, and I got the job.'

The newly elected TD for Limerick East made an immediate impact. James Dillon, who would clash with O'Malley in the

Dáil over the consequences of free education, was an early admirer. 'Dillon was a great friend of my father Jack,' English adds, 'and he said to him after Dunnick's maiden speech: "Ye elected a very bright young man with a great future in Limerick. I was very impressed with this Donogh O'Malley." Coming from the other side of the house, that said quite a lot,' English rightly concludes.

English remembers the different aspects of O'Malley's personality: 'You had two Dunnicks really. When he wasn't drinking he was a very shy man, quiet and a bit distant. On the other hand, if he was having a few jars he'd be the life and soul of the place. People go on and on about his so called drinking escapades, what he did in the Glentworth, a fight he had at the Brazen Head and so forth.'

'That's only rubbish. Of course like any man fond of a drink, he had a few problems but they have been exaggerated and embellished in a most ridiculous way. I have to agree with Jack [Bourke] that Dunnick found it difficult to socialise after giving up the drink. He was so full of life and energy that I'd say he missed the release and relaxation he got from a few drinks.'

Tom English comes from an avid Fine Gael tradition. However, like Tom O'Donnell, he points out that O'Malley transcended the conventional divide in Limerick East politics. 'I couldn't speak highly enough of him,' English says. 'I came to manage the Savoy in 1954 and you couldn't but like the man. Sadly, I never saw him play rugby. He was long gone from the game at that point, but by all accounts he was a highly accomplished player. His representative record attests to that.'

According to English, the legacy of O'Malley is beyond

154

dispute. 'He introduced the Celtic Tiger. His free education paved the way for it. I am in no doubt whatsoever about that.

'We used to send out navvies with a cardboard suitcase held together with twine, and a pair of wellingtons. If they were very fortunate they might have a pair of shoes. Now they're going out on jets with laptops and pinstripe suits. They can thank Dunnick for that. He had foresight combined with a rare intelligence, and you can't manufacture that.

'I knew Hilda well. She used to go into Jack Bourke's for coffee. I found her very easy to talk to but she was quaint in the way she spoke about certain matters. She'd say, for example, "They bring mares from America to Ireland to get the right bloodlines; they bring greyhounds from Dingle to Belfast so that the right bloodlines will match up. But when we get into bed all bloodlines go out the window." How right she was.

'Fianna Fáil treated her dreadfully after her husband died. When the by-election came shortly after his death, she was in complete shock when they approached her. Certainly she wasn't ready for it. In the next general election, Dessie put his name forward and that was that.

'The only man to support Hilda when all the others turned their back on her was the 'Jackser' Sullivan of Hospital, to give him his due, the reason, of course, being that Dunnick made the Jackser with the buses. And he made a lot of other Jacksers around the country. Even so, Sullivan had the courage and decency to say, "I'm supporting Hilda."

'My father, a dyed-in-the-wool Fine Gael man, went into her office and made a small donation to her election campaign. She had her office near where the Belltable Theatre is now located. I voted for Hilda. Daragh, to a certain degree, came of age during the campaign. He made a speech outside Todds in O'Connell Street, and for a young fella aged fifteen he was brilliant. The speech was very much off the cuff but he got a great response. He was a chip off the old block certainly and I suppose he had a bit of the actor in him even then.

'I was immensely proud of him that night, and we became great friends after. And wouldn't you know it, like his father, he had an uncommonly good memory and is very bright as well.

'We seem to have forgotten the contribution that Dunnick made during his political career. The foundation he put in place for the Ireland we have today has too easily been brushed under the carpet. You had to be impressed by the man, irrespective of your politics.

'I'm convinced he would have gone on to lead the country, and he would have done it well. When you take the likes of a Dunnick and compare him to what is going on in politics nowadays, you have to wonder: where have we gone wrong?'

16

Three Key Dates
in the History of Modern Ireland

Con Houlihan says he is too young to write his memoirs. He may have already produced them over the course of a writing life. Reading, writing and conversation are serious matters for the Castleisland, County Kerry, native; that's not to say that he takes himself too seriously. 'Sure what do I know?' he asks, as he drifts into a welter of topics and opinions that touch on a hundred and one things, pouring out in a ceaseless flow from his gifted mind.

Only when he is writing, reading or speaking does he find that complete absorption where all sense of time is lost: looking up from the pages, thinking it is still morning. He discovers it is early afternoon and that the untouched tea has gone cold.

Many years ago, Houlihan discovered that the way he read had to change to comply with his growing consciousness, an awareness that he will not live forever, and that all human life is essentially in the same fix. He questioned the accepted tenets and succeeded in thinking them out for himself. Certain books that mirrored not just the story but reflected something close to his own life and the society in which he lived became dear to him. The quality of the writing supplanted the quality of the material whence the story emerged and was shaped.

Houlihan lives an examined life and there is a tenderness toward the weak and unfortunate with an almost feminine sensitivity to human suffering.

'When I was doing my MA in UCC (1948-9) some of the books were not available in the college or local libraries, but they were to be found in the National Library in Dublin. This meant I had to go up and down to Dublin about once a month. Many's the time I'd be sitting on the steps outside the National Library, and it was there I came to know Charlie Haughey, Garret FitzGerald and Hilda. They were a very bright generation. I didn't get to know Donogh until later years, but I knew him from playing rugby.

'Long ago, Tralee Rugby Club used to have a big festival meeting, with teams from Tralee and several from around Kerry. Quite a few players on these teams played their rugby in Limerick. That's where I first saw Donogh playing rugby. He was a good player, maybe not a great player. He could be a bit fancy but he was tough.

'I suppose he was a bit of a show-off but he could surely play the game. I'd call him a flair player, but more essentially a good ruck player. His best position was Number 8 in the second row. He played for three provinces, and an argument could be made that he was good enough to play for Ireland. The war put paid to that and we'll never know. No doubt he was a tremendous athlete but I suspect playing international rugby for Ireland was not a big priority for him.

'"He wasn't able to express the song of his loneliness." I used this line by the Italian poet Giuseppi Ungaretti in the programme notes to the first Luke Kelly Memorial Concert in May 1984.'

The line clings more tenaciously to the late Minister for Education. Houlihan has an innate understanding of big men, men who were larger than life and undiminished in death.

The big Kerryman learned his rugby in the tough junior leagues with his native Castleisland, and the scars are still there from the unruly rucking and the cheap shots. Sitting in a pub one day, Paddy Kavanagh turned to Houlihan and said, 'You know nothing about poetry,' a cheap shot that merely bounced off the Kerryman. Houlihan smiles when he reflects on that comment: 'I took it as a compliment. Sure he'd have known wouldn't he?'

Kavanagh would have known jealousy, especially when it came to those in his vicinity who were being published. Houlihan can write with equal facility about poets, painters, bogmen, sportsmen and sportswomen, musicians, horses, travellers and road bowling.

Michael Mills was another person who sensed the loneliness beneath O'Malley's joking and merriment, the feeling that Ungaretti alluded to. Nonetheless it would be unwise to conclude that O'Malley had a premonition that he was close to death. 'I've read that and heard it said all right,' Houlihan says, 'but I don't believe it for one moment.

'In any case, he was one of my heroes, and I'll tell you why: Daniel O'Connell began the momentum of constitutionality, and that was kept going by Davitt and Parnell. We came into the twentieth century on a tide of non-violence, a vision well articulated by Arthur Griffith. Forget 1916; that took us back into political violence and that strangely has endured to the present day.

'I'm ambivalent about Pearse. *The Irish Times* ran a series headed "The Legacy of Pearse". Well, I was reared to revere Pearse, but I feel like putting it in one phrase: "The Legacy Of Omagh." The physical violence has been inculcated; you can't blame him, there were many others down to the present day. And there's no guarantee that it's gone away, far from it.'

Houlihan points to three key dates in the history of modern Ireland. 'You have Dublin 1913, the year of the Lockout. That would be the first landmark. The workers learned the benefit of solidarity; that was the start of the real trade union movement. My father was involved with the founding of the first branch of the ITGWU in Castleisland. Jim Larkin has been appropriated to a certain extent by many writers, and sure, what of it?

'The next landmark was 1948, the year Noël Browne became Minister for Health in the Coalition government. He took away the blight of TB; that was his contribution to Irish life. Before his time, if your doctor told you had TB you gave up, you said: "I'm going to die," and a lot of them did. He taught people to have hope and not to lie down. And he proved it; within four or five years sick people I knew who thought they were going to die were walking around. That belief became more and more part of life.

'People thought TB was hereditary; if one member of the family got it, they all got it. Maybe it was contagious and maybe it wasn't, but it was mentally contagious. Because of what Browne did to banish the mythology associated with TB, his contribution can never be overestimated.

'Donogh O'Malley introduced free secondary education in 1967 and that was the third landmark in modern Ireland. He forced this measure through against fierce opposition. They were saying we couldn't afford it. He was hated by members of his own Party. The civil servants would have had him assassinated, such was the hatred and opposition, not to mention the wrath of Catholic Church. I would say Archbishop McQuaid despised Donogh, and sure why wouldn't he? Donogh was a threat to the status quo, the lucrative hegemony of the Church in education, and he wasn't a bit timid about calling them out.

'He broke the green bureaucratic tape and the opposition of the Fianna Fáil Party. He was relentless and he was tough, and he needed to be. He got the Bill through; to me that Bill was the making of modern Ireland. By this I mean that thousands of boys and girls in the mountains were now able to get to school because of the buses. Many of these went on to tertiary education. Their contribution to our present wealth, such as it is, was considerable.'

17

John Healy on the 'Wild One'

John Healy's first encounter with Donogh O'Malley was after O'Malley had been summoned for drunk driving and an escape clause was provided by a closed sitting of the court – the infamous Haughey secret courts. O'Malley was given a £25 fine and there was no publicity. Quite a few Fianna Fáil supporters availed of this private hearing system. Healy got wind of it and ran it on the front page of the *Evening Mail*. The story also appeared in a Backbencher column in the *Sunday Review*.

When O'Malley discovered who was responsible he confronted Healy: 'Are you the fucker that crucified me in the *Mail*?' Healy indicated defiantly that he was, whereupon O'Malley invited him to have dinner with him. Healy maintains that the incident changed both their lives for the next six years. 'He had got so much sympathy from his colleagues over the exposure that he vowed "no bastard in a newspaper will ever get that chance again," and overnight stopped drinking.

Healy idolised O'Malley, and in turn O'Malley (along with Brian Lenihan and Charles Haughey) leaked morsels of Cabinet information to Healy, who skillfully conveyed this in his Backbencher column. They spent long hours in O'Malley's flat. What O'Malley truly felt about Healy cannot be gauged. He may have used him for his own ends, but they enjoyed each other's company and O'Malley admired the conviction of the Mayoman.

The Backbencher column, a collaboration between Healy and Ted Nealon, changed the direction of Irish political journalism. Gone was the tedious verbatim reporting of Dáil speeches; in its place Healy provided commentary, insight, gossip and lively discussion about politicians and their constituencies. After the demise of the *Sunday Review,* Healy's column moved into *The Irish Times* and ultimately became 'Sounding Off'. It was exclusive to Healy and he was allowed considerable leeway by *Times* editor Douglas Gageby to indulge his prejudices.

Healy, at times wrote intuitively, eloquently, and two of his books, *Death Of an Irish Town* and *Nineteen Acres*, have endured and are invaluable for an understanding of the passing of small-town, small-farming life in the west of Ireland.

The day O'Malley died, Healy called a friend and cried uncontrollably. Twenty years later, he wrote a two-part profile of O'Malley for *Magill* magazine, published for the anniversary of O'Malley's death, in March and April 1988. Much of what he wrote was heartfelt, but Healy's facility for arranging events and statements to embellish his story is very evident.

John Healy's profile of O'Malley is compelling and emotive and reveals Healy at his best: candid, contentious and with a flair for the dramatic. Healy used a spare, direct style to portray his subject.

However, there is nothing of historical merit in the profile; all the anecdotes, incidents, strokes, fights, and passionate debate have been well documented. It is an entertaining read but it is also contrived, tendentious and rather arbitrary in its choice and sequence of events.

Healy, of course, was economical with the truth in creating his point of view. There is a tension between the tale-telling and the shape-making and it is the shape-making that prevails. Nevertheless, it is worth having another look at the wild one depicted in his profile.

The main thrust of Healy's piece is that O'Malley was a man in hurry because he was running out of time. Healy implied that the minister was aware of his impending death and hindsight allowed him to allude to various utterances and gestures, premonitions of death. One of these was O'Malley's gift to him in 1967 of his bound copies of the *Dáil Debates* covering his career in Leinster House. 'You'll find some use for them,' he said gruffly that night. 'The hoorin' things are no use to me.'

In the early 1960s Healy, Desmond McGreevey, Arthur Gibney, Brian Lenihan and Noel Mulcahy would gather around O'Malley each night for a late dinner in the Martello Tower restaurant in the Intercontinental Hotel. O'Malley was Parliamentary Secretary to the Minister for Finance and had charge of the Board of Works. It was a relatively minor position but it gave O'Malley power.

He took control and insisted that the final decision on all issues was his. He clashed with the civil servants, who were not accustomed to being roared at and bullied. Much to their chagrin, conventional procedures were dispensed with and decisions were accelerated and manipulated. The wild one prevailed despite a series of confrontations and disruptions caused by Fine Gael TD Oliver Flanagan.

Donogh O'Malley vindicated Lemass's decision to promote him from the backbenches. In his first year he shattered the budget estimates with a spate of building, reclamation, and other schemes all over the country. He included Fine Gael deputies in this largesse, knowing the value of a letter sent to the local paper in response to that constituency's TD. Every public penny spent brought relief to individuals, parishes, and communities.

Lemass approved of O'Malley's brash, confrontational style and used him to good effect. O'Malley's first full ministerial position was in Health, and the same dynamic approach rattled cages in various quarters. O'Malley made himself accessible to junior doctors and especially nurses and training nurses. He opened all letters marked personal and contacted the writer, usually by phone. He became hugely popular, creating a growing sense that he was a man who got things done quickly by overriding the bureaucracy.

Healy supplies a version of that infamous day in the Dáil when O'Malley was late for an important vote, and time has not diminished the sense of theatre and drama surrounding it. There was a critical vote on the greyhound coursing bill and it was expected to be a very close call. O'Malley was in the Dáil bar when the division bells rang. There was a general movement toward the chamber but O'Malley lingered in the belief that he had enough time before the doors were closed.

He barely missed the closing doors, after which no one was admitted. What happened next is the stuff of legend. He arrived at the chamber door nearest the Taoiseach, and began to rattle the door, then charging at it and finally kicking it shouting: 'Open this fuckin' door.' Keeping a straight face in that situation was beyond the House but de Valera and Lemass maintained a quiet delight as the onslaught continued. The Ceann Comhairle rang the bell and the deputies made their way through the division lobbies.

This sustained outburst by O'Malley saw him hauled in by Dev for what many thought would be at the very least be a severe dressing down.

'They tell me you are drinking again, Donogh.'

'I wouldn't mind them, Taoiseach – sure, Jaysus, they told me you used to sleep with Mary MacSwiney and I never believed them.'

De Valera was so startled that he entirely forget the purpose of the meeting with O'Malley, who emerged from the Taoiseach's office grinning mischievously, to the exasperation of colleagues. When asked what Dev said to him O'Malley replied, 'The Chief told me he never slept with Mary MacSwiney.'

Increasingly, Healy found himself alone in the company of O'Malley, sometimes three or four nights a week, never leaving O'Malley's flat at 12 Eglinton Road before three in the morning. O'Malley, well into sobriety, would offer drink, but endless pots of tea was the drink of choice. Three hours later O'Malley would be up and poring over the morning newspapers. Indeed it was customary for O'Malley to read the country editions of the morning papers before going to sleep.

Healy believed that he was responsible for pushing O'Malley in the direction of free education but points out that the minister's interest in education went back many years. They certainly argued about the economic and social impact that free education might have on the standards in secondary schools and the political consequences.

Healy captured Lemass's ploy of using O'Malley to fly a kite by breaking the news of the scheme rather than putting the proposal to the Cabinet. Delivering the free education speech to a gathering of the National Union of Journalists was another master stroke, ensuring massive and widespread publicity.

After the speech in Dún Laoghaire Healy met up with O'Malley in El Greco restaurant. The early editions of the Sunday papers gave the speech comprehensive coverage, with the certainty that all three Dublin dailies would make it the lead story on Monday morning, accompanied by supportive editorials.

'I drove him back to the flat later,' Healy wrote. 'He put the kettle on and while we waited for it to boil, the excitement of the night still hyping him, he said, 'You know what I did tonight, Toro?'

'Yes I do: you've just finished sixteen years of Fianna Fáil rule.'

The big smile and then: 'Unless of course, Fianna Fáil meets the challenge of a young educated electorate.'

Healy ended part one with characteristic hyperbole. 'The speech was not six hours old, but both of us knew that a great new Ireland was born that night.' Once again the brandy was forsaken and they toasted the night and the future with tea in elegant china cups.

Healy began the second part of the profile on a peculiar, dissonant note.

He wrote that the week of Donogh's death in March 1968 was the worst of his life, not only because he had lost a great friend, but because Ireland and the Irish people had lost an irreplaceable politician and person. His Backbencher column for the following Saturday took on an air of unreality in the form of a phone conversation with Donogh. It might have been appropriate in 1968 but twenty years on it rings hollow and doesn't work.

The countrywide popularity that O'Malley attained was not lost on Healy. 'In rural Ireland he was lionised as Minister for Education. The sons and daughters of smallholders now had an open door to second level education. 'Get an education and you can travel the world,' was a saying in most homes in the west.

'The scheme killed the hated [county council] scholarship system. They were limited in number and tended, more and more, to be the prerogative of teachers' sons and daughters who were specially tutored so as to win them.'

Healy knew little about Hilda O'Malley and it's not clear if he ever met her. When Donogh was appointed to a full ministry it was expected that Hilda would join him in Dublin: 'O'Malley, however, held her hostage to, and in, Limerick, fearing that to bring her to Dublin would start a round of sneerings that O'Malley was "like the rest of 'em as gets a state car – he moves house to Dublin where we can't reach him."' He wasn't the first political husband to make his wife hostage to the constituency and won't be the last.

'His phone bill was mighty, apart from the rent he paid in Eglinton Road, a flat large enough to accommodate the whole family. In fact they used it during visits to Dublin or on the very odd weekend when O'Malley had to stay in Dublin for some Cabinet business. He had to relay the news of the day to Hilda and get the political news of Limerick in return.'

This is how Healy described Donogh O'Malley's death:

'He came off the platform, leant against the state Mercedes and said he didn't feel too well. When he collapsed a woman brought a glass of brandy but, knowing he had sworn off it, asked Con Houlihan, his driver, if it was safe to give it to him. Con said if she didn't, it wouldn't matter, he wouldn't survive.

'O'Malley swallowed the brandy and looked at Con and said: "Con, I should never have given up the fuckin' drink."

'On the dash to Limerick, he asked them to open the windows to let fresh air in. The nurses did their best but when they had reached the hospital; in his beloved Limerick all they had was the big frame of Donogh O'Malley. His great and generous soul had escaped to its Creator and all that live-long day and into the evening Masses, a shocked people would gasp at the news and would weep openly and unashamedly for it sensed, in the instant, the nation's loss and that it was irreparable.'

Healy was incensed by the way Hilda was treated after Donogh's death: 'Hilda would have been a suitable candidate and in the first days after his death she was the favourite. In Fianna Fáil, widows were generally picked if they were willing and Hilda was willing. Some senior Cabinet people did not care for her candidacy and Donogh's nephew Desmond O'Malley was declared the favourite of a rump of the Party in the city. The struggle was quite bitter. The city would see men who carried Donogh shoulder-high when he returned to Limerick with his first ministerial post and who crowded into the Brazen Head with him, desert his wife in the nominating hour.'

18

WHAT IF?

Historians are divided as to the value of counterfactual history. There is a considerable element of snobbery and elitism among those who frown upon what one historian referred to as 'an extravagance of the imagination'. Be that as it may, Irish history is for many a living thing, to be discussed and picked over time and again. The facts of what happened don't change but to concede to the purists would decimate the vibrancy and choke the life out of Irish history and its many personalities.

What if Donogh O'Malley had lived for just two more years? His nephew Desmond would not have entered politics as the family law practice continued to flourish. Hilda O'Malley would likely have accepted the Fianna Fáil nomination since her children were two years older. Those are the immediate implications. What would have happened to his good friend Charles Haughey? This is the most interesting 'what if' question in light of the events of the late 1960s.

According to Tony O'Dalaigh, 'Donogh was close to Charlie, close to Brian, Neil Blaney to a lesser extent, but not to Kevin Boland, and definitely not to George Colley. George and Charlie, coming from the same constituency, were avowed enemies. There was history and bad blood between those two. Charlie was by far the cleverer guy. He was brilliant in school. George by comparison was bright, a fluent Irish speaker, but more of a plodder. Charlie would have totally outshone him at school.

'Donogh was worried when Lemass retired. His fear was that Colley was going to get the leadership. Of the fourteen ministers in Cabinet, George and Charlie were very junior and would have ranked in the last four. Charlie was hopeful about his prospects until Donogh told him he had no chance whatsoever as he wasn't popular enough. Charlie clearly took that advice on board; he suspected that Donogh knew what he was talking about and trusted his advice. Jack Lynch took over, after trouncing Colley in a pointless contest.

'I have to say that in all my time with Donogh, I never heard him say a bad word about Charlie. Donogh had political wisdom. I think he might have controlled Charlie better. He certainly did in the contest with Colley. He'd have been a wise head in relation to the Arms Crisis. I can't imagine that he'd be going importing rifles! He never evinced that kind of mad republicanism that Charlie had. Moreover, Donogh was a very pragmatic politician all through his career.

'Haughey always had a thing about people coming from the North, about the RUC and the way they handled people, and there was a real smouldering 'fuck those' attitude. I saw this again when I was Director of the Royal Hospital, 1986–90. He came on a visit as Taoiseach on one occasion and he asked me, 'Why do we have portraits of Charles and all them fuckers up there?'

'Haughey, without a doubt, was the person who missed Donogh most. There was a good understanding between them and Charlie lost more than just a friend. No one can explain what Haughey was doing in the O'Malleys' house the evening of Donogh's death. He came to the house and left quickly and mysteriously. Ten years on it scarcely mattered. Everything had changed so rapidly in relation to the North.

'I sometimes wonder how Donogh would have dealt with situations and people up there. He had charm and charisma, was an accomplished rugby player and President of the FAI, all of which might have made him a bit more acceptable in some quarters.

'He would have relished dealing with the likes of a Maggie Thatcher. A long-time admirer of the oratory of former Fine Gael leader James Dillon, O'Malley was among many who made time to listen when Dillon was speaking in the Dáil. When a performance was called for Dillon delivered.

'O'Malley would have made a very constructive contribution to the crisis in the North. After all, he became the first Dáil minister to enter the Stormont Parliamentary chamber in June 1965 as part of the Lemass-O'Neill meetings. Donogh was Minster for Health when he met his counterpart in Belfast and he took gleeful delight in upstaging his colleagues.'

Would O'Malley have gone on to become Taoiseach? John Healy didn't believe so. He maintained that Donogh didn't have the temperament to become the leader of the country. The received wisdom says that he was brilliant in Cabinet but unsuitable for the top job. This is based on a perceived personality defect and does not stand up to scrutiny.

O'Malley captured the imagination and won the hearts of the nation with his work in health and education. His achievement – and his legacy – was based on an unerring pragmatism. His political astuteness was underestimated; this was largely his own doing, and he wasn't perturbed about it.

No convincing argument can be made that O'Malley was not Taoiseach material. When he died, he had just begun to achieve what Kavanagh in 'If Ever You Go To Dublin Town' called 'his potentiality'.

They say that Thomond Park is the spiritual home of Munster rugby. There is also a profound sense of O'Malley's spirit around Thomond and its neighbourhood. The Brazen Head, a pub he fought in, and later purchased, is still a rugby establishment but cosmopolitan when it comes to sport. The powers-that-be in Munster rugby might acknowledge in some way their indebtedness to O'Malley when the refurbishment of Thomond Park is finished.

Jack Lynch, it seems fair to say, would have found O'Malley a contentious colleague. But If O'Malley could endear himself to both Lemass and de Valera, there is every reason to believe that the former hurler and the former rugby player would have worked together amicably. The soft-spoken Lynch would have handled O'Malley in the same way he dealt with the great Limerick hurlers, the Mackey brothers – for whom he had the utmost respect – on the playing field.

Lynch was well able to handle himself when opponents tried to rough him up. He could punch as quickly and as hard as an accomplished boxer. In a match between Cork and Limerick in the 1940s, John Mackey was playing full-forward on Frank Murphy [former President of the GAA] who was full-back. Lynch was having a blinder in midfield and Mackey decided to go out and do something about it. Shortly after he came back to his position with a bloody nose.

'What happened you?' asked Murphy.

'Lynch hit me,' replied Mackey.

'What happened?'

'He told me I had no business out around the middle of the field.'

'Serves you right,' said a smiling Murphy.

Sport would remain a huge part of Lynch's life, and the respect he had for O'Malley's sporting accomplishments was well known. After O'Malley's death he addressed the Dáil:

> From his student days it was evident that political life had a special appeal for him, and that he in turn, had, in the highest degree, the talents and personal qualities which public life demands…Donogh O'Malley gave generously of himself to the last, in the constant advancement of the causes and ideals to which he was dedicated. What he accomplished in public life will remain a fitting monument to his memory.

Speaking at the graveside of W.B. Yeats in 1965, Frank O'Connor observed that 'in the summing up of any man's achievement there are two things to be taken into account – the man's character and the character of the circumstances he had to deal with.' He believed, with Yeats, that Everyman's work, whether it be literature, music, politics, sport or anything else is always a portrait of himself.

The *Limerick Leader* of Saturday 16 March 1968 spoke of the untimeliness of Donogh's death:

Our tomorrows will be emptier....

His death seemed to make a mockery of the bright spring sunshine that flooded O'Connell Street and that rather austere building in Marlborough Street that housed the Department of Education. He sat there, a big man, his volatile personality filling the place. He would talk of politics, of Limerick, of the years not so long ago.

In the same way that John F. Kennedy was tragically taken from us in the flower of a brilliant career, Donogh O'Malley's untimely passing leaves many questions unanswered. But then he had achieved much in his relatively short time in two ministerial roles.

Limerick liked and loved this big man with the smile. He was a sportsman – and Limerick cherishes its great rugby players, past and present, as much as Cork loves a good hurler, or rugby player, for that matter.

19

CHARLIE, DESSIE
AND CREATURES MADE OF CLAY

> Politics is not the boy scouts! It's a bit of a haul.
> And I think, per se, it has to be: you've got to sort
> of win your spurs and fight your way through…
> It's a long hard haul: most of the guys who
> are at the top have served out a pretty tough,
> demanding apprenticeship…I could instance a
> load of fuckers whose throats I'd cut and push
> over the nearest cliff, but there's no percentage in
> that. (C.J. Haughey, *Hot Press* interview, 1984)

Reliable sources on the origins of the O'Malley political
dynasty are scarce, but a cursory glimpse into the history of
the family is instructive. Donogh O'Malley was a product of
the merchant prince, elite of Limerick society.

Psychologists – and one must be wary here – have
debated the concept of the charismatic leader, whether the
individual becomes so by nature or nurture. Charisma may
or may not be a true talent, but it is certainly innate, shaped
and refined by learning experience. It is perhaps a true gift
of nature. O'Malley was charismatic, handsome, possessing a

larger-than-life personality. As John Healy points out, he was someone who would have been a success in any walk of life.

What distinguished O'Malley from his peers was his accessibility and his possession of the common touch. He was at ease in any social setting, be it among the bourgeoisie of the Ennis Road or drinking with his labourer pals on the Dock Road. It was inevitable that Charles Haughey would be drawn to this man; he cultivated a close friendship with him, sought his advice (especially so in the succession stakes after Lemass resigned) and respected it.

Haughey may have felt he was destined to lead the country, but he needed O'Malley to refine the imperfections in his make-up. He warmed to the tall, athletic, and self-assured Limerick man. While O'Malley was unpredictable, Haughey was more shrewd, even devious, surviving on his political acumen and intellectual prowess.

The friendship between the two men was mutually beneficial. O'Malley was able to say and do things others might only dream about, and Haughey gained a measure of self-confidence from being in the company of his political colleague. He had none of the advantages of his friend; he came from unremarkable stock, and he aspired to create the aura that his background denied him.

What he did have, however, was resilience, especially after his political exile following the Arms Crisis. That Haughey had to contend with Dessie O'Malley, nephew of his close friend, newly installed to the front ranks of the Cabinet as Minister for Justice, was an outlandish not to say ironic role-reversal, unrivalled in modern Irish politics.

It became even stranger when Dessie threw in his lot with the erstwhile outcast to form a coalition government: then the attempted heaves and intrigue, the quest for leadership, and the dénouement that left both men on the periphery.

'EXEGI MOMUMENTUM'

Thus Horace began the last poem of Book III of his *Odes*. 'I have erected a monument,' he said, 'more lasting than bronze, a monument by which I shall ever grow fresh with posterity's praise.' An arrogant prophecy perhaps, yet two thousand years later, it is being fulfilled, the strange paradox being that it lives through the medium of a dead language.

The City of Limerick has embraced the exploits of Mick Mackey in hurling and Richard Harris in film and theatre. Fitting pieces of sculpture are prominently located in the city centre. There is no tangible acknowledgement of O'Malley apart from a local authority housing estate (of ill repute) named after him and a wing of the University of Limerick.

This would scarcely matter to the wild one as his legacy cannot be quantified. He opened the door to gifts of the mind for subsequent generations. It is to the folk memory one must go to understand the magnitude of his enduring monument. Folklorist Dáithí Ó hÓgáin, himself a County Limerick man, sums up his contribution:

> He had a very strong personality which was tempered by independence of mind and a fine imaginative flair. These were the qualities that brought free education, which helped substantially to level the playing pitch for the youth of Ireland from different social categories; and they were qualities which would conceivably have brought about many other good and progressive things had he lived.

Very few public figures have this combination of talents, and when they do they always leave their mark for the better on their society. Donogh O'Malley is, for these very same reasons, well established in the folk memory, especially in Limerick city and county, where many anecdotes are told of his generous and sometimes flamboyant style.

Contrary to received wisdom, the past is not a foreign country; it is all around us, shaping our present. Architecture, painting and sculpture are the most tangible presence of the past, while music, although invisible, is the most real and accessible to many people. Literature – words – is the most common presence, the keeper of our civilisation, its values and attitudes.

History enables us to recover the past, to revise it and reinterpret it. Literature, however, is a living history of our human awareness, allowing us access to the feel of things rather than their meaning, the essence of what it is like to be a human being in any time, in any place.

> Only twenty miles to go and I'll be
> Home. Seeing two crows low over the land,
> I recognise the land's uncertainty.
> The unsensational surrender and
> Genuflection to the busy stranger
> Whose power in pocket brings him power in
>   hand.
> Realising now how dead is anger
> Such as sustained us at the very start
> With possibility in time of danger,
> I know why we have turned away, apart
> (I'm moving still but so much time has sped)

From the dark realities of the heart.
From my window now, I try to look ahead
And know, remembering what's been done and
    said
That we must always cherish, and reject the
    dead.

Brendan Kennelly, 'The Limerick Train'

SELECTED BIBLIOGRAPHY

Boland, Kevin. *The Rise and Decline of Fianna Fáil*. Cork: Mercier Press, 1982.

Browne, Noël. *Against The Tide*. Dublin: Gill & Macmillan, 1986.

Collins, Stephen. *The Power Game*: Ireland under Fianna Fáil. Dublin: O'Brien Press, 2001.

Coogan, Tim Pat. De Valera: *Long Fellow, Long Shadow*. London: Hutchinson, 1993.

Cooney, John. *John Charles McQuaid: Ruler of Catholic Ireland*. Dublin: O'Brien Press, 1999.

Dwyer, T. Ryle. *Short Fellow: a Biography of Charles J. Haughey*. Dublin: Marino Books, 1999.

Farrell, Brian. *Seán Lemass*. Dublin: Gill & Macmillan, 1983.

FitzGerald, Garret. *All In A Life*. Dublin: Gill & Macmillan, 1989.

Healy, John. *Nineteen Acres*. Galway: Kennys Bookshop, 1978.

Horgan, John. *Seán Lemass: the Enigmatic Patriot*. Dublin: Gill & Macmillan, 1997.

Joyce, Joe. *The Boss: Charles J. Haughey in Government*. Dublin: Poolbeg, 1983.

Kavanagh, Peter. *Beyond Affection*. New York: Kavanagh Hand Press, 1977.

Lindsay, Patrick J. *Memories*. Dublin: Blackwater Press, 1992.

Manning, Maurice. *James Dillon: a Biography*. Dublin: Wolfhound Press, 1999.

Mills, Michael. *Hurler on the Ditch*. Dublin: Currach Press, 2005.

O'Shaughnessy, Denis. *How's Your Father? Stories Of Limerick*. Limerick, 2002

Quinn, Antoinette. *Patrick Kavanagh*. Dublin, Gill & Macmillan, 1989.

Stack, Tom. *No Earthly Estate: God and Patrick Kavanagh*: Dublin: Columba Press, 2002.

Stuart, Francis. *Black List, Section H*. Illinois: Feffer & Simmons Inc., 1971.

Walsh, Dick. *Des O'Malley, A Political Profile*. Dingle, County Kerry: Brandon Books, 1986.

REFERENCES

pp. 36, 38: Peter Kavanagh, *Beyond Affection*. New York: Kavanagh Hand Press, 1977.

pp. 37–9: Antoinette. Quinn, *Patrick Kavanagh*. Dublin, Gill & Macmillan, 1989.

pp 57: *Limerick Leader*, 15 July 1959.

pp. 68–9: Seanad Éireann, Volume 61, 25 May 1966.

pp. 71–3: Bruce Arnold, Extracts from 'Southern Society Today', Paper to the Annual Conference of the Irish Association, Carrickfergus, 14 November 1999.

p. 74–5: John Healy, *Magill*, March 1988, p. 47.

p. 80–1: City of Limerick VEC minutes, 29 July 1966.

pp. 81: (suspension of Limerick VEC): *Limerick Leader,* 4 January 1967.

p. 79: T.K. Whitaker on free education quoted in John Horgan, *Seán Lemass: the Enigmatic Patriot*. Dublin: Gill & Macmillan, 1997, p. 298.

pp. 83–84: John Horgan, *Seán Lemass: the Enigmatic Patriot*. Dublin: Gill & Macmillan, 1997.

p. 84: 'No one is going to stop me', *Seanad Éireann*, 9 February 1967.

p. 88: McQuaid quoted in John Cooney, *John Charles McQuaid, Ruler of Catholic Ireland*. O'Brien Press, 1999, p. 385.

p. 94: Extract from 'free education' speech, Royal Marine Hotel, Dun Laoghaire, Saturday, 10 September 1966.

pp. 94–5: personal communication from Dáithí Ó hÓgáin to the author, 2007.

p. 96: statement of the Minister for Education, 18 April 1967.

pp. 97-9: Patrick J. Lindsay, *Memories*. Dublin: Blackwater Press, 1992.

182

p. 105: *Limerick Leader*, February 1968.

p. 108: memo from Tony O'Dalaigh to Donogh O'Malley, 8 March 1968, in the possession of Tony O'Dalaigh.

p. 117: Emily Dickinson, 'It was not death, for I stood up'.

p. 119: Robert Hayden, 'Those Winter Sundays'.

pp. 161–8: John Healy, *Magill*, March and April 1988.

p. 173: Frank O'Connor, 'Graveside [centenary] Tribute to W.B. Yeats,' *The Irish Times*, 14 June 1965.

p. 175: Charles J. Haughey, interviewed by John Waters, 'Personally Speaking', *Hot Press*, December 1984.

p. 177: personal communication from Dáithí Ó hÓgáin to the author, 2007.

pp. 178–9: Brendan Kennelly, 'The Limerick Train', *Old Limerick Journal,* 31, 1994.

Appendix

Speech by Donogh O'Malley, Minister for Education, to the National Union of Journalists at the Royal Marine Hotel, Dun Laoghaire, on Saturday, 10 September 1966

I have been asked to speak to you to-night about current economic objectives and how education can help in realising them. The choice of subject has been thrust upon me, and I shall avoid boring you by simply recommending those of you who are truly interested in the role education can play in achieving economic objectives to read the survey team's report 'Investment in Education', and the annexes and appendices thereto. The price from the Stationery Office is thirty-five shillings – and I am happy to tell you that at that price it is a best-seller.

As the incoming Minister for Education, I would prefer to speak to you tonight about the role of education in the development of the future Ireland.

It is rather fortunate that I should be making my maiden speech as Minister for Education before a body of journalists. For authors, journalists and publishers are, especially to-day, an important part of the educative system of any country. The press, radio and television wield a powerful influence in these days of mass communication That is why I am hopeful that these media, and you who influence them so much, will support in every way possible the new plans which I shall be unfolding for our developing education services.

To understand the problems with which we are confronted in education, we must look a little into the past.

In the course of the present century, the history of this country has been a story of political resurgence, of cultural revival and a successful fight for independence.

Those things which are of lasting value were dearly bought by a preceding generation. An astonishing effort – intellectually and physically – took this country across the threshold of independence.

At the beginning of this century, national objectives were basically few. We could not have afforded the luxury of diffuse aims. We regarded political freedom as the first essential of progress, and the wisest, bravest and best our people consciously dedicated their lives to this ideal – to a final conclusion of terrible beauty

There were other manifestations of revival. The Irish language was being taught and learned increasingly. Irish music and literature were reaching exciting levels throughout the country The Abbey was a new and stimulating experience. These were tributaries which fed the mainstream of thought which was focused on release from political bondage.

This was not, however, a risen nation marching proudly to its destiny. This was not the vow of the people, conscious of their strength and demanding their rights. This was the work of a handful of men who knew painfully what had to be done These were men who had thought deeply about themselves, their neighbours, their community and the abstractions of their nationhood These were men who felt things which the main body of their countrymen did not feel and did not understand. These, in fact, were the men who bore in themselves the conscience of a nation.

It is a matter of history that independence created as many problems for us as it solved. There was a crisis of political stability; a civil war; an economic war; a depression; a world war. The economic measures which were eventually adopted in the early thirties needed time to take effect, and they were disturbed by the second world war

The ideals which defeated an empire were, sadly, not fully appropriate in the new situation. The idealistic emphasis had shifted from the political to the economic. The new slogans were productivity and the standard of living. The pressing problems were unemployment and emigration. These were – and still are – problems which are not susceptible to dramatic solutions.

There is no Jordan for us to cross, no land of milk and honey within easy reach. We should not require of our leaders the ability to strike water from rocks. We are not, however, in the desert. In the intervening period, we have succeeded in establishing political stability, in reducing the flow of emigration and in bringing the standard of living to an improved level, and our population is increasing.

We are unshackling ourselves gently from the chains of the past. What of the future? What is demanded of us? And, what can we hope for?

We have an economy which is basically sound, provided we husband our resources carefully We have recently had some difficulties and some disappointments. Much of these have stemmed from sources beyond our control – international shortage of capital; foreign inflationary trends; balance of payments difficulties abroad, especially in Britain, resulting in the Levy.

Some of us seem to be easily discouraged by temporary reverses.

We are not a nation which can deploy substantial financial resources. We must allocate resources as priorities demand. Productive investment must come first. Investment in education must get priority, for it is a form of productive investment which is vital not only to our future economic development but to the entire national fabric of the growing nation.

We are, it must be constantly remembered, living through an era of change. Many of the former assumptions on which we based our lives are being questioned. Community relationships are changing. They are changing between country and town; government and governed; employer and employee; and they are breaking down the old class structures. Underneath the surface stability of the nation are forces and ideas, beginning to work like leaven, which must bring about immense changes before many of us are gone from this scene.

And, in step with this interplay of ideas, of forces of intellect and thought, education must move with the times it is meant to serve. The world of to-day and to-morrow will give scant attention to the uneducated and those lacking any qualification. We will be judge [sic] by future generations on what we did for the children of our time.

Education, as an eminent statesman said in the last century, makes a people easy to lead but difficult to drive; easy to govern but impossible to enslave. Education is not a mere process of preparation for a good job: it is more a means of ensuring that we provide the future citizens of the nation with an educational system which will give them the means of developing as a mature and adult people in a world of continually-increasing challenges. We live to-day in a world of the mass media -a world in which it is impossible to shut out the influences that motivate people throughout the globe.

Some of these influences are good, some banal. And only a people educated in the full sense of that word will be able to recognise the true values, to accept and adapt the intrinsic that is new, and discard the dross that is merely novel. Only an educated people in the future Ireland can take their place in the full comity of the nations and yet remain distinctively Irish.

I am fortunate in entering office when there is a consciousness as never before of the vital part education must play in the future of the nation. I bring with me, as announced by An Taoiseach in Dáil Éireann, a government assurance that education is to receive priority. Priority is going to mean exactly what it says – as I hope the events of the coming years will show.

Before I speak of problems, let me count my blessings. I have succeeded two Ministers for Education, Dr. P.J. Hillery and Mr George Colley, who have done so much in laying plans for the future, the results of which are coming daily to fruition. I have inherited a system of education which contains within itself the necessary elements of flexibility. Above all, I have under my Department a devoted band of teachers.

There is, of course, a lot remaining to be done with our education system. And I am convinced that we must attack the fundamental weaknesses in that system on a full national scale. And we must begin right away.

There is no difficulty in picking out the basic fault in our present educational structure – and that is, the fact that many of our families cannot afford pay even part of the cost of the education of their children.

I think it is one of the great tragedies of our history since independence that we have not found the means to check this terrible loss to the national potential for economic and cultural advancement.

Every year some 17,000 of our children finishing their primary education do not receive further education. This means that almost one in three of our future citizens are cut off at this stage from the opportunities of learning a skill, and denied the benefits of cultural development that go with further education.

This is a dark stain on the national conscience. For it means that some one-third of our people have been condemned – the great majority through no fault of their own – to be part-educated unskilled labour, always the weaker who go to the wall of unemployment or emigration.

I believe that this is a situation which must be tackled with all speed and determination. And I am glad that I am able to announce that I am drawing up a scheme under which, in future, no boy or girl in this State will be deprived of full educational opportunity – from primary to university level – by reason of the fact that the parents cannot afford to pay for it.

I have always been concerned with the dilemma of parents, particularly those with large families, who, in the matter of post-primary education, wish to do their very best for their children but who find that the school fees – even when these are modest – are quite beyond their means.

I propose, therefore, from the coming school year, beginning in September of next year, to introduce a scheme whereby, up to the completion of the Intermediate Certificate course, the opportunity for free post-primary education will be available to all families.

This free education will be available in the comprehensive and vocational schools, and in the general run of secondary schools. I say the general run of secondary schools because there will still be schools, charging higher fees, who may not opt to take my scheme; and the parent who wants to send his child to one of these schools, and pay the fees, will of course be free to do so.

I propose that assistance towards the cost of books and accessories will be given, through the period of his or her course, to the student on whom it would be a hardship to meet all such costs.

I intend, also, to make provision whereby no pupil will, for lack of means, be prevented from continuing his or her education up to the end of the Leaving Certificate course.

We must, also, face up to the position of making financial aid available to the pupil who, because of the location of his home, can have post-primary education available to him only if he enters a boarding school.

Finally, there is the university level. While I do not at this stage wish to say anything which might cut across the recommendations of the Commission on Higher Education, I cannot let the occasion pass without referring to the plight of the pupil who has reached a good standard in the Leaving Certificate examination but who, due to the inability of his parents to pay, cannot proceed to a university or other course of higher education. We must, and we will, come to the assistance of such a pupil. I, therefore, propose to put in train shortly the working out of a scheme to cater for such cases.

The officers of my Department are now engaged in the detailed statistical work that is necessary in drafting and bringing to completion such a revolutionary change in our approach to the provision of education for our people. I hope to be able to give the Dáil the completed details of these schemes when I come to introduce the Estimate for my

Department before Christmas.

The importance of providing better-educated young people in our developing economy makes this 'free education scheme' all the more urgent. Already, a shortage of skilled workers is apparent in some sectors of our industry. Very soon, that shortage will be acute, and could endanger economic progress – unless we move quickly into the age of technology.

Our universities present us with a very big problem indeed. For one thing, universities are of their nature extremely expensive, Another thing is that our present university set-up is a legacy of history – and history is a stubborn wrestler. However, as you know, the Commission on Higher Education is engaged at the moment in preparing a plan. Until it speaks, I prefer to remain silent on the larger issues of the universities.

I have decided, however, that the problem of university overcrowding must be tackled at once, and shall, therefore, very shortly give the green light to Dublin and Cork for the building plans which they have put before me. I am, also, giving consideration to the difficulties of University College, Galway.

And now, I gather, a lot of people are highly interested in hearing my views on the Irish language. Well, I have not come to the post of Minister for Education to preside over the obsequies of the national language.

I personally deplore the current trend of bitterness over the Irish language, and I seek no involvement in it. Instead, I would appeal to all who care for the language to rise above barren controversy. We must get back to the spirit of the early revival – to the days when Irish men and women were glad of the chance to learn the language: when the appeal was to the patriotic instinct.

The language is not the property of any group or organisation. It belongs to us all as a people. This week, we celebrate the 750th Anniversary of Ballintubber Abbey – the Abbey that refused to die. There is an analogy here for those who wish to ponder on it.

If we, in this generation, allow the language to become a political plaything, or to become the preserve of any organisation or group – no matter how well-intentioned – then, we might as well be honest with ourselves, and throw the language on the scrap-heap.

We have a wonderful opportunity at this moment to get the language movement back to its earlier place in the hearts of our people. This opportunity comes with *An Buntús Gaeilge – Foundation Irish*.

This, in short, is a simple and ready way of encouraging the revival of Irish as a colloquial tongue. It boils down simply to this – learn 900 words and phrases, and one can converse widely in Irish.

This new method is available through the work of my Department, in cooperation with An tAthair Colmán Ó hUallacháin of the Irish Franciscan Fathers, who, with their great history of Gaelic scholarship, are ideally fitted to such an enterprise.

The development of this new method of learning Irish has opened a vista in the language scene. For this reason, we, as a nation, must give it every support.

Foundation Irish provides the opportunity for improving and streamlining the present system of teaching Irish in the schools. Likewise, the methods applied can be adapted to provide a more efficient method of teaching English, something urgently needed in our schools. We shall, through the new methods and less stress on grammar, be able to reduce the number of hours allotted to the teaching of Irish and, at the same time, obtain more beneficial results.

Already, the *Buntús* method in Irish teaching has been tried out in a number of schools. This year it is being followed in some 150 primary schools and fifty secondary and vocational schools. The results so far have fulfilled our highest expectations. Committees, with representatives from the various teaching organisations, are at work in my Department preparing new textbooks and teaching aids, based on the *Buntús* method.

But it would be a pity if the Department of Education, which now has the means to give a new and vital impetus to the aim of extending the general use of colloquial Irish, were to confine this to the schools.

Accordingly, I am arranging that the *Buntús* method of teaching the language shall be made available in the fullest way possible for the general public. A special textbook for adult use is being prepared by the Department. I hope to arrange with Radio-Teilifís Éireann for courses in the *Buntús* method starting next year. And I am hopeful that I will have the support of the daily and provincial press in making this new means of acquiring fluency in Irish available to their readers.

These, then, are some of the broad avenues of development along which I see our educational system moving – moving towards the goal of becoming fully effective and attuned to the needs of the nation in the years ahead.

I see these developments as an essential part of the investment we shall be called on to make if we are to keep faith with ourselves and hand on a worthwhile inheritance to the generations to come. All in all, I visualise these plans as being a national commitment to education.